Consulting in Uncertainty

The traditional model of consulting places an emphasis on diagnosing a problem and finding a cure. But in today's business world of globalized organizations, rapid knowledge proliferation, and the intertwining of economies, that approach is becoming less and less viable; problems are quickly redefined, new knowledge (and ownership of that knowledge) is constantly surfacing and being challenged, and no solution is permanent. *Consulting in Uncertainty* articulates a model of consulting that addresses the uncertainty and interconnectedness of the world in a post-industrial knowledge era.

Emphasizing outcomes and inquiry over "diagnosis," Brooks and Edwards outline this new consulting model, as well as the skills consultants must bring to the table in any uncertain and dynamic environment. Integrating practical knowledge with scholarship, this book covers skills such as:

- Relational skills and the consulting relationship
- Cultural awareness and related skills
- Contextual analysis
- Facilitating inquiry
- Collecting and efficiently analyzing data or information

Consultants and students of consulting, as well as managers, teachers, counselors, and even parents, will find this book enlightening and useful in navigating today's uncertain world.

Ann K. Brooks is currently Professor and Director of the doctoral program in Adult, Professional, and Community Education at Texas State University, USA. She worked for ten years in industry and education in Asia and Latin America prior to taking a position at the University of Texas at Austin, where she co-founded the Human Resource Development Leadership Program at the McCombs School of Business. Dr. Brooks is the author of over fifty research articles and books and her research on adult learning and human resource development has received numerous awards. Most recently she was the recipient of the "Cutting Edge Award of 2009" for the Academy of Human Resource Development as well as the "Best Paper of 2007" for the Human Resource Development Quarterly. She co-edits the Adult Education Quarterly. In addition, Dr. Brooks has provided consultation to organizations in the U.S., Australia, Cambodia, South Korea, Japan, and Afghanistan. She recently returned from Cambodia where she was a Fulbright fellow. Her current research interests include immigration and work, race/ethnicity, learning and transformation in work organizations, and consulting. Dr. Brooks received her doctorate from Teachers College, Columbia University.

Kathy Edwards is a faculty member in the Management Department of the McCombs School of Business at the University of Texas at Austin, USA. She has taught in both the MBA and the undergraduate business programs for twelve years and currently teaches a course in Consulting and Change Management. Dr. Edwards is the recipient of numerous academic awards including the UT Regents Award for Outstanding Teaching, Texas Exes Teaching Award, and the Harkins Foundation Award for Effective Teaching in Business. Dr. Edwards is the Program Chair for the Management Consulting Division of the Academy of Management. In addition to her work as a faculty member, Dr. Edwards has held leadership positions in business, non-profit and governmental organizations and entrepreneurial ventures. An experienced consultant, the training and consulting firm Dr. Edwards founded just celebrated its 24th year in business. Her current research interests include consulting and facilitation in work organizations. Dr. Edwards received her Ph.D. in Adult Education and Human Resource Development from the University of Texas at Austin.

Consulting in Uncertainty

The Power of Inquiry

Ann K. Brooks &
Kathy Edwards

Routledge
Taylor & Francis Group
NEW YORK AND LONDON

First published 2014
by Routledge
711 Third Avenue, New York, NY 10017

and by Routledge
2 Park Square, Milton Park, Abingdon, Oxon OX14 4RN

Routledge is an imprint of the Taylor & Francis Group, an informa business

Library of Congress Cataloging-in-Publication Data

Brooks, Ann (Ann K.)
Consulting in uncertainty : the power of inquiry / Ann K. Brooks & Kathy Edwards.
pages cm
Includes bibliographical references and index.
1. Consultants. 2. Consulting firms. I. Edwards, Kathy, 1950–
II. Title.
HD69.C6B756 2013
001—dc23
2013017580

ISBN: 978-0-415-80048-8 (hbk)
ISBN: 978-0-415-80049-5 (pbk)
ISBN: 978-0-203-15262-1 (ebk)

Typeset in Minion
by Apex CoVantage, LLC

For Howard and Linda. Thank you for your support and patience.

Contents

List of Figures, Tables, and Boxes

Figures

Tables

Boxes

Acknowledgments

All creative efforts are collaborative, and this book is no exception. We would like to acknowledge the many people who contributed to our thinking.

Thank you to consultants Linda Donelson, Gilda Garcia, Tim Garripa, Lynne Gilfillan, Namisha Kachhla, and Matt Kouri, who generously shared their experiences with us, and colleagues John Burrows, Doug Dierking, and Pam Haunschild for providing feedback.

Editor John Szilagyi inspired us as well as served as a consistent source of practical information.

Brooks thanks Rachel Brooks-Ames-Lachenmeier, Sophie Brooks-Ames, and Marsha Congdon for the many conversations about the challenges of being both a consultant and a client. She would also like to thank Kayon Murray and Geleana Alston for their feedback and editorial help. Appreciation goes to all who have shared their learning with her, including Elizabeth Kasl, Joanne Sandler, Karen Watkins, Luise Ahrens, Margaret Bywater, Miguel Guajardo, Oscar Mink, Neth Barom, Robert Hazen, Lee Sang Seub, Ly Monirith, Victoria Marsick, and too many more to name.

Edwards offers appreciation to all her students at the University of Texas at Austin for everything they have taught her. The students in her Consulting and Change Management class are her inspiration for this book. Students provided invaluable input into this effort throughout the process. Thank you also to Jana Birchum, Marc Clapp, Darlene and Larry Dean, Iris Harrell, Charlotte and Cheryl Ingram, Deanna Olson, DC Wengelnik, and Susan Word for feedback. She would especially like to thank Linda Gayle Edwards for sharing encouragement and expertise.

Introduction

The role of the consultant is one we all take on throughout our lives. Whether or not we formally call ourselves consultants, we consult to family, friends, and colleagues. We also consult as part of our professional work.

The challenge for all of is to evolve our practices to address the often confusing challenges of living and working in an era characterized by a proliferation of knowledge and information, making our world more uncertain than it has always been, and by the increasing interconnectedness of the world. Not only are we rapidly sharing our cultural knowledge and forms, a development that is both exciting and alarming to many around the world, but our economies are ever more intertwined, a fact that many economists point to as contributing to the increasing gulf between the rich and the poor, both across and within nations.

So in this book, we begin to articulate a model of consulting for a postindustrial era. It is an era distinguished by constantly evolving knowledge produced collectively in response to an ambiguous and uncertain world. Organizations are spread out across the world, and work and learning have moved beyond the bounds of the workplace as the ties between workers and the workplace have frayed. The notion of owning knowledge is challenged, protected, and contested in the courts, as our societies try to make sense of the "leakiness" of the Internet, as well as the threat such open sharing of knowledge and co-creation of new forms presents to those who would hang onto power and or who wish to preserve traditional cultural forms.

With such rapid proliferation of knowledge and the shifting of some of the economic and cultural boundaries that have distinguished the idea of nation states, a consulting model that takes into account the increasing uncertainty and interconnectedness of our world is needed. Similarly, a model of consulting is needed that incorporates the idea that, as in any sustainable business, consultants must deliver on what is promised to clients.

So this book begins to articulate a model of consulting fit for a postindustrial knowledge era. It is based on research, theory, and our own and other consultants' and clients' experiences with working together both locally and internationally to make organizations and communities function better.

The book is written for anyone who consults with others and would like to hone their consulting skills. This includes MBA and undergraduate business majors, students and professionals from fields such as psychology, education, communication, or government, and the professors who teach them. It will be of particular interest to professionals in the fields of human resource development, organizational development and human resources, all of whom play a consultative role every day. It may also be useful to experienced professionals who consult in their own fields, those who are newly hired to work for consulting firms, and practicing consultants looking for new insights and ways to improve practice. Finally, managers and leaders of organizations such as corporations, non-profits, and NGOs may benefit from the focus on inquiry and consulting.

The Work of Scholars and Practitioners That Informs This Book

The inquiry model of consulting described in this book places learning and inquiry, knowledge, and outcomes at the center of consulting work. The theory and research on which it draws have been developed by generations of scholar/practitioners. The term *scholar/practitioner* signifies an important distinction from the popularized sharp dividing line between scholars and practitioners, since scholar/practitioners, mostly from professional schools in universities, work both in various parts of the community and in universities, floating back and forth together with students, faculty, alumni, and community members while addressing real-world challenges.

We will identify some of the scholar/practitioner theory and research informing this inquiry model of consulting.

John Dewey and Learning from Experience

In the early 20th century, John Dewey developed the idea that learning doesn't just come from teachers transferring knowledge to students. Rather, in real life, we are learning all the time, making new sense of our experiences in an effort to better meet the challenges we face. In his book *Democracy and Education*, Dewey goes on to link experience with thinking:

> Thinking is the accurate and deliberate instituting of connections between what is done and its consequences. It notes not only that they are connected, but the details of the connection. It makes connecting links explicit in the form of relationships. The stimulus to thinking is found when we wish to determine the significance of some act, performed or to be performed. Then we anticipate consequences. This implies that the situation as it stands is, either in fact or to us, incomplete and hence indeterminate. The projection of consequences means a proposed or tentative solution. To perfect this hypothesis, existing conditions have to be carefully scrutinized and the implications of the hypothesis developed—an operation called reasoning. Then the suggested solution—the idea or theory—has to be tested by acting upon it. If it brings about certain consequences, certain determinate changes, in the world, it is accepted as valid. Otherwise it is modified, and another trial made. Thinking includes all of these steps,—the sense of a problem, the observation of conditions, the formation and rational elaboration of a suggested conclusion, and the active experimental testing. While all thinking results in knowledge, ultimately the value of knowledge is subordinate to its use in thinking. For we live not in a settled and finished world, but in one which is going on, and where our main task is prospective, and where retrospect—and all knowledge as distinct from thought is retrospect—is of value in the solidity, security, and fertility it affords our dealings with the future.[2]

These ideas provide a philosophical grounding for the later development in the mid-20th century of various forms of action inquiry, including action research, participatory action research, collaborative inquiry, and action learning. These methodologies differ in some of their assumptions, particularly moral and political,[3] but they each incorporate the basic ideas about knowledge, learning, and experience that were laid out by Dewey. To paraphrase and quote Dewey again, the phases in the cycle of inquiry are: (1) the need to act in an incomplete or indeterminate situation; (2) the proposal of a tentative solution tempered by reasoning about what might happen if it is enacted; (3) testing of the suggested solution by acting on it; (4) determination of whether it brings about certain consequences, certain determinate changes, in the world, in which case it is accepted as valid. Otherwise it is modified, and another trial made. We use the term "phases" rather than the more linear "steps" or "stages" because phases points to the potentially nonlinear process of both experiential learning and action inquiry.

For consultants, these ideas provide both a philosophical framework and wealth of methodological tools for creating and, importantly, *implementing* new knowledge within the specific contexts of our clients.

Later Developments: Activity Theory

Contemporaneous to both Dewey's work in the U.S. and action inquiry, both in the U.S. and worldwide, was the work of activity theorists in the Soviet Union,[4] and later in Scandinavia[5] and the United States.[6] Activity theory is more of a framework for understanding learning than it is a predictive theory. This body of theory pointedly places learning as occurring as *a part of practice* within *specific cultural, historical, and social contexts.* Thus, knowledge is not a generalizable "thing" that can be "installed" regardless of context. These theories also highlighted the roles of *activity* oriented toward an *object* or *subject.* For consultants, that object is the client's hoped-for outcome. In our current world, "context" may mean a local and contained culture, such as those studied by Jean Lave,[7] an early pioneer of activity theory—or more often, "context" may mean the mish-mash of intersecting and overlapping cultural influences characteristic of business, international organizations, and increasingly, academia.

In the world of consulting, this means that "off the shelf" and "scalable" products risk being both irrelevant and inappropriate across contexts. It also means that we *must* bring in the context-specific knowledge of our clients. We *must* focus on an object or outcome, and we *must* engage in contextualized activity with our clients if we are to actually deliver the implemented outcomes for which we have contracted. We cannot parachute in carrying our expertise, drop it, and leave it to our clients to implement.

Client-Consultant Relationships and Neuroscience

In the "business" of consulting, relationships are often characterized as transactional: pay for service rendered. Words floating in the consultant literature such as "client resistance" and "influencing clients" as well as the abundance of derogatory words for consultants in the popular literature suggest less of a partnership and more of an adversarial relationship. The ubiquitous references to "building trust" and "lack of trust" seem to seal this conclusion.

In contrast to this, the fields of organizational development and process consultation[8] have theorized and developed methodologies to emphasize the centrality of relationships to client and consultant success.

Many observers would say that all we have to do is look around and we can see the ways that we affect each other interpersonally, in teams, in organizations, in communities, and indeed, across the world. In this book, however, we draw particularly on recent research in neuroscience, which seems to provide convincing evidence of the ways in which humans are, indeed, social beings. Much of neuroscience research supports what the wisdom of practice and previous behavioral research tells us: we cannot build the organizations or communities we want without paying attention to how we affect each other, as well as to the quality of the relationships we foster. Specifically, neuroscience tells us that our emotions affect our ability to change, emotions are contagious, thinking and emotions are inseparable, and the plasticity of our brains means that the choices we make have a direct bearing on who we become.

Outcomes, Not Problems

Problems have long been the focus of consultant work. They have also occupied scientists. We draw on the work of practitioner-scholars who have developed assets mapping,[9] and the many who have contributed to appreciative inquiry.[10] The focus on assets has even begun to emerge in the consulting literature.[11] This does not mean that problems don't exist or that consultants need to pretend to be blind to them. Rather it emphasizes what the organization or community already has in terms of competent, hardworking, and well-intentioned human resources, structures, and policies. Looking for problems in organizations and communities invites resistance among employees and community members. Most of us think we're doing the best we can, and being targeted for overhaul undermines our identities and forces us into a defensive posture: resistance.

We emphasize outcomes for three reasons: (1) we owe it to our clients to stick with them until we deliver what they've paid us for; (2) a focus on outcome or goal invites the knowledge and resources already present in the organization or community to be brought to bear on the challenge; and (3) outcomes direct our primary attention to building the future rather than repairing the past. Knowing the better place we're headed is far more motivating than fixing what's wrong. It invites creativity and the efficient use of available resources.

The Ethics and Morality of Consulting

Prepublication reviewers for this book told us that we need to include a chapter on ethics. This is important advice since much of the criticism leveled at the consulting industry has been a moral indictment that boils down to, in business terms, "consultants take money and client knowledge without providing the service they were paid for."

Businesses, including consulting firms, have been the focus of much moral and ethical critique. This has resulted in more interest on the part of the business sector in social responsibility and the "creation of shared value." Michael Porter and Mark Kramer pointedly describe in the *Harvard Business Review* the view that has become widespread in the media, on the streets, and the workplace:

> The capitalist system is under siege. In recent years business increasingly has been viewed as a major cause of social, environmental, and economic problems. Companies are widely perceived to be prospering at the expense of the broader community . . .[12]

In other words, businesses often overlook their dependence on and interconnectedness with the communities and world from which they draw resources and sell to people.

As consultants, we can only ask, are we contributing to this?

Taking responsibility for helping our clients define actionable outcomes forces this point. We can clearly know at the outset whether our work will put hundreds of others out of work, destroy the environment and livelihood of a community or, in fields like education and health care, turn what were sectors committed to the public good into profit centers disciplined by systems focused on return on investment rather than human growth and well-being. We can then make a conscious and ethical choice about whether or not we will do the work.

Beyond getting clear about the ethics of what our clients hope to achieve, we can also look at our own motives. As one long-time consultant with one of the large consulting firms observed about firms like her former employers,

> [They are] large consultancies that hire MBAs straight out of school and arm them with spreadsheets, pro forma methodologies, incoherent jargon, and a not-small amount of arrogance. I blame these people for conceiving and propagating the many management myths that are the roots of some of the biggest problems in business today—lack of innovation, short-term focus, obsession with financial gains over creating valuable products and services, and stressed-out, over-worked, disengaged employees.[13]

Consulting is indeed a profession wrought with ethical and moral dilemmas. However, in this book, we don't specifically focus on these issues. Rather they are integrated into the book in the acknowledgement of our interconnectedness; the contextuality of all of us and our work; and our emphasis on outcomes, inquiry, and implementation. While many of us work from contexts other than the large consulting firms that have been the target of many of the critiques, we can all take heed and look at whether our work is for the common good or just for ourselves. Examining our outcomes and staying with our clients through implementation push us to examine whether we are providing value for money and to look at the effects of our work for people, organizations, communities, and beyond.

Brief Overview of the Book

Part I describes the inquiry approach we take to consulting, lays out the model of inquiry consulting, and highlights the attitude or stance a consultant working with this model brings.

Part II examines the relational skills that consultants who engage in consulting as inquiry need. Specifically, we look at emotional skills; at becoming aware of and taking responsibility for the quality of relationship we develop with our clients and colleagues; and importantly, at the particular demands of working with clients and colleagues in international contexts and from cultural backgrounds different from our own.

Part III looks at how we facilitate inquiry as consultants, how we go about learning enough about our clients' contexts to make our work relevant and appropriate, and finally, at the nuts and bolts of collecting information or data and then analyzing what we have gathered in useful and efficient ways.

Part I

Rethinking Consulting as Inquiry

Consultants are knowledge workers. We draw on both our education and our experience to help our clients. But in an uncertain world, is that enough?

Humans have always looked to those who know more, have more wisdom, or have more experience to help us find our own paths through the world. In traditional societies, elders or spiritual leaders have played that role. As societies became more complex, religious and educational institutions developed to guard and transmit that knowledge. In our current world, we draw on all of those sources as we try to figure out how things should be done or, often, how they should be done better.

Educational institutions have traditionally treated learning as the transmission of knowledge and skills from those who know more to those who don't yet know as much. This tradition is embedded in the form of a teacher at the front of the room and the process of testing to make sure students "got it." Increasingly, though, these habits of educating are coming under fire. As it turns out, particularly in the world of professional education, this "telling/testing" model is not very effective. Students may "know" more about their chosen profession and have sharpened analytic skills, but when they start to practice, they have a tough time applying all of the knowledge. This is especially true in a world that defies both our tradition-based and our science-based predictions of the future and our hope that one setting is pretty much like another and so what worked here will work there, too. Our world is both uncertain and culturally complex.

What we count on, though, is that humans are learners by nature. We naturally seek out the best information and then try it for ourselves. If the best information comes from watching someone else do something, then we take what we observed and adapt it to our own bodies, our own cognitive gifts and limitations, and our own situations. If the best information comes from the Internet, an educational institution, or an expert, we go get that information and then figure out how it can work for us in our situation.

Consulting at its least effective adopts the "tell them" model. Whether we bring a proprietary process that we or our company has developed or an off-the-shelf training package or process, or simply try to sell what we learned in graduate school, we are ignoring the ability of our clients to participate in finding better ways to do their work.

Part I lays out an understanding of consulting that assumes our clients' abilities to innovate ways to get to the outcomes they want and the role we can play in helping them do it better.

Chapter 1, "Changing the Consulting Story," elaborates on how the "tell them" or advice model differs from an inquiry model of consulting. We challenge the model of consulting as problem oriented and reliant on consultant knowledge and the application of expert knowledge to our clients' worlds. Instead, we suggest a shift to outcome-oriented consulting that draws on a client-consultant collaboration aimed at producing innovative, context-specific new knowledge.

In Chapter 2, "Shifting to An Inquiry Model of Consulting", we lay out, step-by-step, what the process of consulting would look like from an inquiry perspective.

This shift requires consultants to adjust the stance we take as we work with our clients. Chapter 3, "The Consultant's Stance," looks at the kind of person we become in our interaction with our clients. Joining together with our clients in inquiry challenges us to relate to both our own expertise and our clients in different ways. Many of us ground our confidence in our own knowledge and try to communicate our own competence to our clients through sharing our knowledge with them. When we shift to inquiry, though, we are not only drawing on our expertise in a specific body of knowledge and know-how, such as engineering or human resources, we are also inviting our clients to join with us, drawing on whatever knowledge and know-how is available, to come up with better solutions. The upsides of this approach are not only better outcomes for clients, but enhanced learning for consultants.

1
Changing the Consulting Story

Everyone is a consultant. We don't have to be employed by an international organization, travel the world, or work with Fortune 500 companies—every time a friend or family member confides in us about an issue with which they are struggling, we are consultants. When colleagues ask us what we think about a problem they are facing, we are consultants. When a member of our team asks for input on part of a project, we are consultants. When a customer or client in any profession seeks our help, we are consultants. And of course, when we or our consulting companies are hired by a client in an organization to advise them, we are consultants.

In other words, each of us is in a consulting role any time we do not have direct responsibility for the outcome, but are asked to help. This book is about what we can do to be most helpful to those who turn to us, no matter the setting.

The Advice-Givers

For many, consulting is about experts giving advice. Box 1.1 shows some of the common definitions of this term.[1]

Box 1.1 Definitions of a consultant

- "An expert who charges a fee for providing advice or services in a particular field" (Encarta Encyclopedia).
- "One who gives professional advice or services" (American Heritage Dictionary).
- "One who advises another, especially officially or professionally: advisor, counselor, mentor" (Oxford English Dictionary).
- "[A] *consultant* is defined as someone who either advises a client—another person or an organization—on the desirability of taking some

action, who assists the client in making a decision and then assists the client in planning or implementing action as determined by the client" (Stroh & Johnson, 2006, 3).

- "By *management consulting* we mean advice-giving to companies provided by trained professionals who help managers solve operational and strategic problems through application of knowledge and systematic analysis of facts" (Fombrun & Oriesek, in Fombrun & Nevins, 2004, 6).

Popular culture provides us with a similar image of consultants. For example, when coauthor Edwards asked undergraduates in a course on consulting to draw their image of a consultant, their most frequent depiction was of someone, usually a man, giving advice in meetings, talking to clients, or making presentations. The consultants were invariably large and their clients were small, and the consultants seemed to dominate their clients. The students also sometimes portrayed the consultant as a doctor, imagining consultants as diagnosing the "illnesses" of and prescribing the "cure" for clients. The story these pictures tell is that a client has a problem ⇒ the client asks the consultant for his or her expert advice ⇒ the consultant gives the advice. Assuming the advice was good and the client follows it, then the happy ending is that the consultant saves the client.

Challenging this image of a benign expert is a strong shadow story that has emerged over the past couple of decades. In this story, the client has a problem ⇒ the client finds a consultant who claims to have expertise ⇒ the client asks the consultant for that expert advice ⇒ the consultant cheats or gives bad advice to the client ⇒ the client suffers. Block notes, only somewhat humorously, that "[t]he first consultant was the Serpent in the Garden of Eden. . . . When Eve followed his advice and picked the low-hanging fruit, the consequences were grave and long-lasting. . . . We still feel the chill of this ancestral shadow cast over our work."[2] Books on management consulting like *Consulting Demons: Inside the Unscrupulous World of Global Corporate Consulting*[3] and *House of Lies: How Management Consultants Steal Your Watch and Then Tell You the Time*[4] tell us that consulting is a buyer-beware market. These critiques range from accusations of overcharging, fad following, cookie-cutter solutions, and lack of results to ethical allegations of lying, cheating, and stealing.

This negative image is powerful, and as Elaine Biech, the author of a number of publications on consulting, has written,

> I was shocked the first time I was called a "beltway bandit"—the term assigned to consulting firms in and around the Washington, D.C. beltway. Since then, I've been called a pest because I followed up too often with a client. I've also

> been called a con man. . . . Some of the negativity is deserved. There are many charlatans in our business.[5]

The consulting profession is not a regulated industry. In addition, most consulting projects are not publicly scrutinized. The potential for abuse exists, as opportunistic snake-oil salespeople operate alongside highly reputable professionals. From this perspective, clients should exercise due diligence in seeking a consultant's help.

The field of consulting is big business. Kennedy Information estimates that the industry as a whole grosses over 200 billion dollars a year worldwide.[6] Unfortunately, many consulting projects are not successful. It is estimated that approximately two-thirds of all consulting projects fail.[7] So the profession still has much room for improvement in meeting the needs of clients.

The Problem with Advice

The tradition of knowledgeable advisors serving as consultants to leaders is as ancient as leadership itself. Kings, popes, presidents, and generals, as well as business leaders and leaders in other fields, have all availed themselves of what Maister, Green, and Galford call "trusted advisors."[8] The search for an advisor or expert appears to be a common human longing. It is a natural response to an uncertain world. From shamans to scientists, from priests to philosophers, from various spiritual guides to business gurus, the world has looked to those who claim to have specialized knowledge to guide us. If our immediate reaction to our own or other people's problems is to seek or give advice, what's wrong with that?

Most of us slip easily into the role of advice-giver; we have learned a lot in our lives. We want to help others, and we personally feel good if we are able to give someone else useful advice. However, as Alger has noted, "We give advice by the bucket, but take it by the grain."[9] For some reason, we are resistant to taking the advice of others. We hear others' advice, and it never seems to quite fit. Somehow, they seem to "not really get" our situation or the complexities of the issues we face, or they think that doing what they advise us to do is going to be easy. What's more, we know that the advice-giver doesn't have to live with the consequences of his or her advice to us, and we're rightfully wary of implementing that advice. And if we watch what happens when we give advice to someone else, we often find that the target of our advice listens closely at first, but the more we advise, the more the listening seems to be "just to be polite." We can listen to others' thoughts about our lives and challenges, but ultimately, we add their advice to everything else we know and come up with our own solution, a solution that fits our situation.

As professional consultants, we are similarly faced with advisees who know their own organization or community better than we do. While we may bring professional expertise or a unique service, each client is unique. All organizations, industries, or communities may share similar patterns, but each has a different history, political and social environment, and constellation of distinct ways of understanding and acting that have developed as responses to a unique journey in this world. These differences mean that what works in one industry, community, or nation is unlikely to work exactly the same way in another.

So it is important to ask how we can better use our expertise to help our clients in their particular contexts. How can we narrow the gap between what our clients want and what we can actually deliver?

Hour by Hour, Moment by Moment, the World Changes

The world of the 21st century is one of uncertainty. We live in a complex and turbulent world in which prediction is difficult, and we have come to see all too clearly the unintended consequences of the actions we take. To add to our increased awareness that problems are neither simple nor clearly bounded and that more than one technically correct solution exists, information and knowledge are transforming at a dizzying rate of speed. The Internet has accelerated the speed of communication and information around the world, and geographic boundaries are no longer barriers to knowledge sharing.

In the midst of such complexity or chaos, the hope that *someone* can tell us the best thing to do with our work, our organizations, our nation, or our money is seductive to us all. Most of us, at some time or another, have felt overwhelmed by the ambiguity in our lives and in the world. We've had to recognize that no easy solutions or answers exist to the problems we face. Nevertheless, who wouldn't like someone to walk into our lives with a simple answer to our problems? We all harbor the hope that someone or something will give us exactly what we want and save us from whatever challenge we are facing.

The advice model of consulting takes care of the anxiety we feel when faced with too much ambiguity. It is grounded in a wish for a closed world in which people can predict what will happen in the future and control all of the variables. It draws on the belief that the world is predictable and we can control the future. But in our most honest moments, we know that

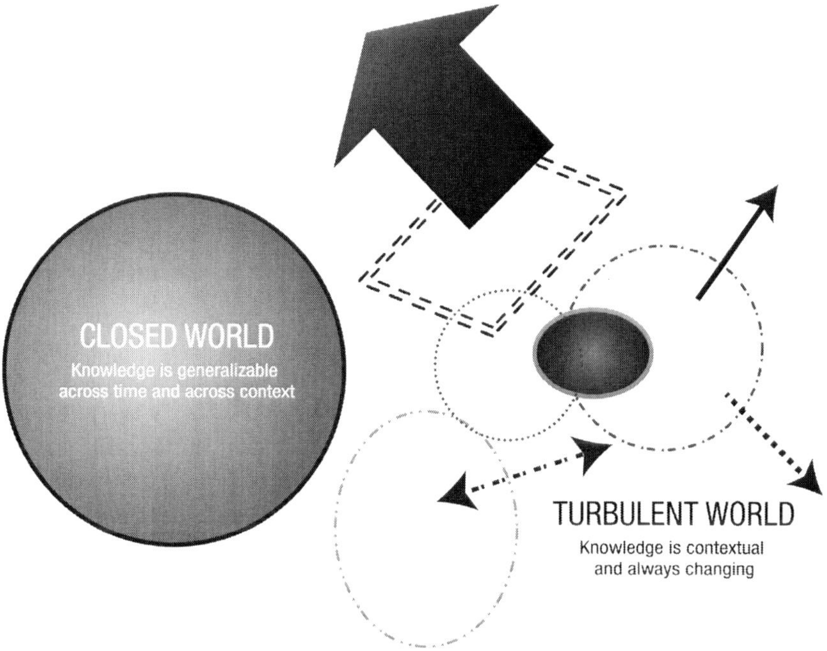

Figure 1.1 Closed versus uncertain world

change is inevitable and the future unpredictable. While we can imagine possible directions that the future might take and try to plan accordingly, in reality we know that anything can happen. The world is neither flat nor closed. We can neither predict the future nor confidently generalize from one setting to another. Figure 1.1 contrasts the serene beauty of the closed world we desire with the uneasiness we feel faced with a turbulent world of seemingly endless and rapid change and countless predictable and unpredictable influences.

So however comfortable both our clients and we might be with a consultant who plays the role of expert knower and advisor—and most consultants assume they are expected to be "the expert"—it is an incomplete role in today's world. And while it may be disorienting to give up our image as expert advice-giver, we can be reassured to know that we can find ways to go beyond advice and be helpful to others.

So What Do Clients Want?

Since so much has been written in the popular press about what clients *don't* want, we decided to review studies conducted by both consultants and scholars on what clients *do* want from consultants.[10] This "market" research, for the most part, mirrors from a positive perspective what much of the literature critical of consultants has been saying.

First, clients want consultants to *deliver outcomes.* They want their consultants to emphasize results and help them to implement recommendations. In this sense, clients want their consultants to actually "make a difference" in their organization or community.

Clients may not be able to articulate the particular outcome they want. Helping them do this is part of our consultant responsibility. So, second, clients want consultants to make sure that both client and consultant clearly *understand the project outcomes upfront* as well as the project expectations and requirements. They want to know what the deliverables will be, and what the criteria for success are. They want consultants who set clear boundaries and scope for the project, and specify who will be responsible for what.

Third, clients want their consultants to *bring and share expertise.* They want new ideas from consultants who come with intellectual curiosity. They want consultants to bring experience, having done in similar settings what they are saying they will help their clients do.

Fourth, clients want consultants who either already *know or want to learn about their clients.* They want consultants to understand and to not overestimate their needs. To that end, they want consultants to gather stakeholder information and input—to consistently communicate with them and senior management and to guide senior management. They want consultants who, during implementation, gather input from employees, consider the impact of change on employees, and help employees deal with change. Most importantly, they want consultants to listen more than they talk in order to work toward solutions that fit the specific client rather than trying to force-fit the client's problem to the consultant's standard solution.

Fifth, clients want consultants to work together with them and increase their own and their organization's or community's capabilities. This means they want consultants who establish a *real partnership* with them, and so do not operate beyond their control. Importantly, working in partnership means consultants ensure that their clients gain new skills from working with them. Clients don't want consultants to make the organization dependent on them for the future.

Finally, but at the heart of everything else they hope for from their consultants, clients want to be able to *trust their consultants' integrity.* They want consultants to share both the risks and the rewards, and to use every skill they have to support their client and push their client forward, even in the face of resistance within the organization. They want consultants who are not motivated by self-interest, who do not have inflated egos that interfere with properly assessing and valuing their client's capabilities. They want consultants who do not take personal gain at the expense of project stakeholders. They want consultants to charge reasonable fees. This is significant since an employee backlash sometimes exists about the high fees paid to consultants, while employees see their own salaries remaining stagnant and cost cuts in their organizations affecting their work and quality of work life. They want consultants who spend enough time on the job. And, they want consultants to be scrupulous about not disclosing sensitive and confidential information.

If, as consultants, we take seriously what clients say they want, what do we need to do differently? If being an expert knowledge consultant, an expert process consultant, or an expert consultant in both knowledge and process is not enough to produce the outcomes our clients need in today's turbulent and diverse world, then what else can we do?

A New Story for a New Era

A new story about consulting is emerging, one that is neither about how brilliant nor how dangerous consultants are. Rather, it is a quieter story—less flashy. It is a story about consultants helping their clients achieve their goals in a world in which all of us, in the words of Robert Kegan, are "in over our heads."[11]

This story could be called the "post-advice model." It is about knowledge, inquiry, openness and partnership. It goes like this: The client wants to achieve a specific outcome ⇒ the client hires a consultant who has expertise regarding how to achieve the outcome ⇒ the consultant and client work together to clarify the outcome ⇒ the client and consultant work together to figure out how to achieve the outcome and then achieve it. This story rests on a different set of assumptions than either the technical or the process expert models.

Shifting the Assumptions of Consulting: From Advice to Inquiry

Consulting as inquiry rests on a very different set of assumptions than consulting as expert advising. Consulting as inquiry assumes that (a) consulting must be outcome oriented rather than problem oriented; (b) consulting must be focused on the co-creation of new knowledge rather than expert knowledge; (c) consultant and client relationships are personal rather than just professional; and (d) dynamic rather than static knowledge is needed in a diverse and uncertain world.

Assumption 1: From Problems to Outcome

The model of consulting as giving expert advice aims to solve problems for clients. Consulting as inquiry addresses problems, too, but the goal of the consulting project is to achieve an outcome. An outcome focuses on a positive future. It is much more energizing to work toward the future than to stay stuck in the problems of the past. Many problems are encountered in the process of working toward an outcome. But keeping our eye on the future focuses our attention on the ultimate goal of reaching the desired outcome.

The advice model assumes that the work of consultants is to identify and develop solutions to clients' problems. An outcome-oriented approach to consulting assumes that the consultant's work is to help clients identify and achieve outcomes, an important criterion for clients in determining successful consultant performance. It is a subtle shift, but one with profound implications.

Focusing on problems rather than outcomes means that the outcome the client wants may never be achieved. Once the problem is named, the consultant can apply a solution, often one that is standard in the industry or sector; once the solution has been applied, the consultant can consider his or her work, for better or for worse, to be completed. Veteran consultant and author Bob Schaffer shares this story:

> A family who had been unhappy for many years about the messy state of various storage spaces in their house heard about a firm of "closet consultants." After a hasty phone call from the family, the consultants arrived on the scene to provide a free preliminary survey. Shortly after that visit a proposal arrived by mail, outlining what the consultants would do with the master bedroom closet. The family initialed the agreement, and within two weeks a miracle was wrought. New equipment was installed, and everything in the closet was tastefully, even artistically arranged. It was a pleasure for the family to witness the transformation, and they willingly paid the consultants' fees. It was a happy ending, except . . .
>
> Within three or four weeks, the closet was just about as messy as it had been before the consulting project. Except for the fixtures that had been screwed into the wall, there was little by which to remember the project.[12]

In this case, the client identified the problem—a messy closet—and brought in the appropriate consultant. However, the consultant applied a solution, one standard in the industry, without really helping the client define more clearly what outcome was wanted. If the project had focused on accessible, organized storage space that met the unique needs of the family, it might have been more successful. That would have led to a whole new set of questions. How often did they use the closet? What did they want in it? Were there things in the closet that the client didn't use?

What things were used most often? What else could have been keeping the closet from staying organized? And so forth.

The assumption that consulting must focus on the outcome avoids many of the pitfalls of looking only at problems. It keeps us from identifying the wrong problem. It keeps us from identifying "the right problem" and missing the nest of problems within which it is embedded. If we are fixated on a single problem or solution, we may fail to grasp the related problems that will quickly rear their heads as we try to implement a solution to our chosen problem—or alternatively, those problems will continue and whatever we implement will have a minimal effect on the identified problem.

Focusing on outcome makes the identification of problems both easier and more flexible. Problems arise, disappear, and change as we track our progress and next steps toward achieving the outcome. Similarly, as both consultant and client learn more, we may revisit the initial outcome goal and revise it. Again, a positive, future-oriented focus provides many potential paths to getting to an outcome. Remember Kennedy's "Man on the Moon" vision. Today collaborative dream teams of cancer researchers and physicians are engaged in their own "moon shots" in a quest to "save lives." Outcomes are being measured by positive patient outcomes, not the number of papers published.[13]

Assumption 2: From Expert to Co-creator of New Knowledge

An advice model assumes that a consultant's expert knowledge is the key to client satisfaction and consultant success. An inquiry model assumes that informed inquiry generated in collaboration between clients and consultants is the best hope of actually creating new knowledge in clients' organizations. Inquiry increases clients' capabilities. What's more, consultants who base their practice on inquiry acknowledge that they cannot possibly know enough about the client's world to be effective. Instead, we come into the client's world open—as inquirers and learners rather than "tellers" or "knowers." We recognize that believing we already know the solution our client should follow can get in the way of learning what is unique about this client and context, and ultimately achieving a successful outcome. It can get in the way of working together to co-create and design custom-fitted innovations together with our clients.

For example, some software requirements engineering consultants question the assumption that the success of requirements engineering projects is based on the consulting teams' technical expertise. Instead, Ian Graham writes, "requirements engineering is about communications."[14]

He goes on to say, "It's amazing how many times I have seen development teams impose their own thinking on a problem and totally fail to understand what the customer is telling them—or more often—implying."[15]

Most of us find it all too easy to impose our own thinking, and we do this for many reasons. The following story, told to Brooks by a management consultant, David, illustrates how even expert and experienced consultants can miss the opportunity to understand their clients through the belief that they already know what is needed.

> David received a call from his colleague Jennifer asking if he would like to do some strategic planning for a local NGO. He had done strategic planning with government and thought this would be a good way to transition into the civic sector. He took for granted that he and Jennifer meant the same thing by strategic planning and that what he understood to be strategic planning was the same as the NGO director's understanding. Without meeting with the director himself, he arrived to work at the appointed time to begin strategic planning with the board of directors. After introductions, he began the work. But it soon became clear that what David understood to be strategic planning was not how the board intended to spend its time. In fact, strategic planning as David understood it was inappropriate for this board at this point in their work together. What's more, the chair of the board and the director of the NGO did not agree on what needed to be done.
>
> As David stood facing a room of board members who had taken time out of their very busy schedules and a board chair and director who did not share the same vision, he broke out in a cold sweat. He thought, "I should have talked with the board chair and the director and maybe some of the board members myself rather than relying on Jennifer's knowledge and understanding of the organization's needs at the time." He realized he did not know enough about his clients and had tried to use an "off the shelf" strategic planning intervention. It didn't fit. He knew he should have talked to the client himself and not relied on someone else to tell him what they needed.

The heart of consulting in a changing world is to work with our clients to seek the knowledge necessary to achieve the outcomes they want, those that are optimal for their particular situations.

As consultants, of course we will bring whatever expert knowledge and experience we have to the table. But we don't have all the knowledge. Clients also bring a wealth of knowledge and expertise about their organizations and their fields to a consulting project, which we need if we are to help them get the outcomes that fit their distinct situations. Through joint inquiry with our clients, drawing on all available knowledge and experience, we can navigate a path from what is unknown—or at best, ambiguous and fuzzy—to the creation of something that uniquely suits each client's goals and challenges.

The advice model assumes that consultants' value rests only on our own expert knowledge. An inquiry model assumes that the consultant also brings the skills of inquiry. This means that we are willing to travel with our clients into their organizational or community world. We don't stand outside, stepping in only to transfer our knowledge or install our service or product. We use every resource and capability available to each of us. We recognize that our expertise alone is not enough.

Assumption 3: From Static to Dynamic Knowledge in Uncertainty

The search for and belief in a universal knowledge has been with us for centuries, with the hope of being able to control our lives and society's and the environment's unruly behaviors. The work of consultants acting as expert advisors is based on this belief. However, as consulting goes increasingly global, the limit to the one-size-fits-all view of knowledge and expertise becomes evident. Culture, context, and moment in history all affect what does and does not work in specific organizations and communities. At the same time, the notion of proprietary knowledge providing a competitive edge is becoming increasingly shaky as the Internet, the movement of employees, international education, and global consulting itself rapidly transport knowledge around the world. It has become increasingly difficult to hoard and sell or to keep secret. Where all this will lead is anyone's guess. But the information and knowledge that consultants have paid for and painstakingly learned is now neatly available and packaged on the Internet. In this world, knowledge itself can no longer justify a consultant's value. Value comes from knowledge *and* something else.

It is comforting to think of knowledge as static. Indeed, the U.S. appears to be devoting considerable energy to transforming its system of education into one that assumes and tests students for mastering static bodies of knowledge. This stands in contrast to efforts being made in other nations to emulate the dynamism that characterized U.S. education for the past century. A story on this phenomenon in the *Chronicle of Higher Education* describes China's efforts:

> Through speeches and policy papers, the Ministry of Education has made clear in recent years that it is unhappy with the widespread use of rote learning and narrowly defined academic programs at its universities. Last year it came out with a 10-year plan for educational reform . . . [that] proposed to introduce Western-style critical thinking and interdisciplinary work.[16]

According to one observer cited in the article, "What they want to see is what happens in a Western classroom, the same lively approach to knowledge, on Chinese soil." To this end, China has brought a campus of Nottingham University to educate students in drug development, stem-cell research, and regenerative medicine; a campus of New York University to build a liberal-arts college, and a campus of Duke University to focus on graduate and professional programs in management, finance, and public health, among others.

In the 21st century, our clients face much more complicated and dangerous challenges than they did 10 to 15 years ago. Socioeconomic trends, markets, seemingly instantaneous innovation by competitors, globalization, mergers across diverse cultures and industries, new forms of distribution, and shifts in national policies have produced ever more difficult problems. Problems amenable to technical solutions are giving way to problems that force us to think in new ways. Our clients need innovative approaches to get where they need to be. In the world of work organizations, the assumption that standardized knowledge can be applied in diverse settings underpins the notion of "best practices." While this may sound appealing, suggesting the simplicity of homogeneity and feeding the illusion of control, no context is exactly like another and conditions constantly change. What works in Detroit is unlikely to work exactly the same way in Cape Town. Thus, as consultants, we have a better chance of helping our clients achieve the outcomes they want if we engage with them in a process aimed at figuring out how to get those outcomes.

Assumption 4: From Professional to Personal Relationships

Acting professionally can often mean acting impersonally. We bring in our expertise, limit our relationship to accomplishing our professional goal with the amount of friendliness required by customer service, and we leave. This professional demeanor can mean that we behave with integrity, but it can also mean that we protect ourselves from the messiness that threatens our sense of control as professionals. We miss much of the information we need to be successful—what we can learn from our clients.

As consultants, we are often working with people and their organizations or communities as they face confusion, uncertainty, and threat. The medical profession has become very aware of the growing impersonal nature of the doctor-patient relationship as medicine has become increasingly fragmented among providers, enhanced by the precision of technology, and oriented toward the bottom line. Books and articles proliferate on how medical education is addressing physicians' communication and relational skills when interacting with their patients. Two emergency room physicians at Brigham and Women's Hospital in Boston and faculty at Harvard University call medicine that is simply the application of technical expertise to patients "cookbook medicine," and suggest it leads to "wrong diagnoses." Instead, they recommend a return to the fundamental partnership between physician and patient, in which the technical expertise of medicine should not be applied without attention to the unique person of the patient. "[I]f you and your doctor are aiming for a diagnosis from the very start," they write, "the attention is focused on you and your story, not just on your symptoms. Instead of forcing you onto a cookie-cutter pathway, your doctor will need to consider each part of your story with you to come up with an answer."[17]

A vice president of diversity at a major university described to us her interaction with a consultant that encapsulates the feeling of professional distance and technical application of expertise, including an ignorance of the relational dimension of consulting:

> The worst feeling there can be is to explain what you need and have the consultant say, "We have this package and it would be perfect for you."
>
> When I took my current job we were 2 years into a contract with this well-known company to develop an Affirmative Action plan. When I talked to them about what I wanted, all they would say is "We do it this way." What they meant is they do it their way. It was problematic for me because they didn't use any higher education data. You have to hear the issue from my perspective, not what fits your paradigm. They think that we don't know what they're doing. It ends up feeling like we've been tricked or duped—and maybe we have.
>
> There has to be a balance between what you bring in the way of experience and expertise, and the ability to see it from my perspective, not yours. That's the worst. I sent the product back to them. They said, "We can give you more consulting assistance, but it will cost you more." When I suggested that we just end the relationship, they were quick to say "We have a contract." The worst part is the actual work still needs to be done and somebody will have to do it.

Consultants cannot afford to treat relationships with clients as impersonal. We have to move from "hired gun" to "partners in crime," as one consulting student put it.[18] The ability to co-create new knowledge requires a close, equal partnership. We need to have relationships that are built on trust, respect, and appreciation for the gifts each of us bring. Inquiry consulting requires a much deeper and more intimate relationship than expert consulting does. We also have to deal with the myriad of emotions that arise for both consultants and clients during the creative process. The quality of our personal relationships with clients can dramatically affect our ability to creatively collaborate together.

These four assumptions taken together underpin an approach to consulting that addresses the limitations of advice-giving. They support consultant and client partnerships, which make possible consultant work that does not just deliver a standard product, an off-the-shelf process, or the same advice we give all of our clients, regardless of their particular context or the unique challenges they face. This is the heart of dynamic consulting. In consulting as inquiry, we center our work on our clients and their success, engaging with them side by side in the complex worlds in which they live and work.

Moving Forward: Partnering in Inquiry

What follows in this book is a model for partnering with our clients to figure out how to achieve the outcomes they want. For the sake of brevity, we call this model "partnering in inquiry." We also refer to it as co-inquiry, and most straightforwardly, as working together with clients to figure out how to get the outcomes they want.

As we lay out this model, we assume each of our readers brings a particular expertise that he or she hopes to share or is already sharing with clients. We focus on how to use that expertise in the service of working with clients to achieve an outcome. We focus on how to structure an inquiry with clients, and on the skills for implementing such an inquiry. We also focus on the particular relational consulting skills that are important in working with clients throughout the inquiry process.

Our challenge as consultants these days is to use our *own* knowledge and expertise as the starting point for an inquiry into what will be most helpful to our clients. Then, together with our clients, we pool our knowledge and draw in the relevant knowledge that is "floating" in the social and scientific worlds around us. Both hazard and promise exist in this world of dispersed knowledge. The hazard is that we will fail to recognize or discover the knowledge our clients and others may have. The promise is that the diversity of knowledge sources and ways of inquiring we can draw on and use together with our clients will help us solve the seemingly intractable problems they often face on the way to achieving their goals.

The hope of this book is to contribute to the conversation that both consultants and clients are already having about how to make consulting more effective. As we all grope forward into an unknown future, this book draws on the combined wisdom and experience of many to articulate a way of thinking about and practicing consulting that can lead to successful outcomes and ongoing inquiry and learning for both clients and their consultants.

In the next chapter, we present a model of the phases of consulting as a partnership in inquiry.

2

Shifting to an Inquiry Model of Consulting

Practical inquiry begins with an end to be accomplished and then searches for means by which it may be achieved.

—John Dewey, *Logic—The Theory of Inquiry*[1]

A model of the consulting process can help us structure our own consulting. At their simplest, models provide us with a series of steps in the process, reminding us of what not to forget as we focus on specific steps. A simple Internet search turns up a wealth of books filled with advice for consultants—advice for the advisors. Although much of the advice available assumes that consultants are experts who sell their advice, some stand out as going beyond that. One book that has been a primer for generations of consultants is Peter Block's *Flawless Consulting.* Block lays out five phases of the consulting process:

1. Entry and Contracting
2. Discovery and Dialogue
3. Analysis and the Decision to Act
4. Engagement and Implementation
5. Extension, Recycle, or Termination.[2]

His description of this five-phase consulting model has provided a welcome roadmap for many consultants.

As the term "process" suggests, the focus is on the human processes of getting a task done rather than on the task itself. Edgar Schein, who has done much to articulate this model, characterizes consultants as engaged in a "helping" relationship with our clients. Focusing on problems, he, like Block, uses medical language such as "diagnosis." Schein advises young consultants to learn as much as they can about psychology, group dynamics, and organizational dynamics. He likens his work to that of an organizational therapist, and indeed, this is not surprising, as his background is in psychology. Schein has contributed much to helping both new and seasoned consultants navigate the tangle of relationships and interests that have such profound influence on the success of any consulting project.

Schein and others' work on human processes in consulting is particularly helpful in reminding us to be attentive to and skilled at considering both human and social dimensions as we work to solve technical problems. We are using the term "technical" here to refer to the complex infrastructure of organizations or societies—for example, accounting, financial, technology, or human resource management systems. Bringing change to systems like these is commonly the goal of consulting contracts. Sociotechnical systems theory suggests that we cannot change such "technical" systems without considering the social systems to which they are connected, and vice versa. Growing out of Eric Trist's and Kenneth Bamford's work with coal mining in England, the theory explains that changing the technical but not the human aspect of an organization tends to increase the unpredictability of the human aspect. Conversely, changing the human but not the technical dimension increases the unpredictability of the technical dimension.[3]

Many studies have chronicled the dysfunction that can unintentionally occur when we change technical systems without thinking about the social systems to which they are linked, or vice versa. For example, one recent study documented how improvements in radiation therapy technology resulted in the diminished role of radiation therapists in the treatment process. Without a trained medical professional acting as an interface between the technology and the patient, technology errors went undetected. The unpredicted outcome of this technical improvement has been the documented increase in the incidence of radiation-induced patient injuries and mortality.[4,5] A technical solution may seem to be the most direct path to an outcome, but this path can still end in failure if we don't think about the human beings and social systems that must implement or utilize them, or that are affected by the change. On the other hand, too much focus on human and social systems may obscure the task that has brought us together in the first place. Neither approach by itself is likely to result in successful outcomes.

Both Block's and Schein's models have been influential for and helpful to practicing consultants. Sociotechnical systems and other theories provide additional lenses for analyzing our clients' worlds and the usefulness and potential impacts of our projects and interventions. However, the model presented in this book is different from process models in that it directs consultant and client work together toward clear outcomes, especially action and implementation. It emphasizes the co-creation of new knowledge, and while incorporating the need for process skills, sees them as being in the service of inquiry aimed at producing outcomes.

We have learned from these models and theories, emphasizing the importance of technical expertise and considering the needs of stakeholders to the consulting project. However, the inquiry model of consulting takes account of the particular challenges of consulting in complex and uncertain conditions with organizations and communities that are simultaneously unique and similar to others around the world. As consultants, our clients are challenging us to produce outcomes, collaborate and partner with them, and make sure that whatever is learned enhances not only our own capacity as consultants, but the capacity of our clients, too. The inquiry model of consulting enables consultants and clients to draw on the knowledge and information as well as the energy, creativity, and analytic abilities that each can bring to the partnership in order to find ways to achieve outcomes. Table 2.1 compares the advice model, the process model, and the inquiry models of consulting.

Table 2.1 Comparison of consulting models

Consultant Emphasis	*The Advice Model*	*The Process Model*	*The Inquiry Model*
What is the Consultant's task?	Solve problem	Solve problem	Achieve the Client's desired outcome
What should the relationship between Consultants and Clients be?	Consultant transfers or delivers knowledge to Client	Consultant and Client work together on human relationships and organization dynamics	Consultant and Client are partners on technical and social/human dimensions of change
Who is the expert?	Consultant is the expert brings knowledge and best practices	Consultant is a "helper" or process expert	Client and Consultant each bring different types of expertise to bear on achieving the outcome
How should the Client's capacity be increased?	Transfer knowledge in the form of product or service	Help Clients learn to more effectively work together	Client and Consultant co-create knowledge needed to achieve the outcome
How much attention should the Consultant give to the uniqueness of each Client organization or community?	Low (knowledge transferable across contexts)	High	High

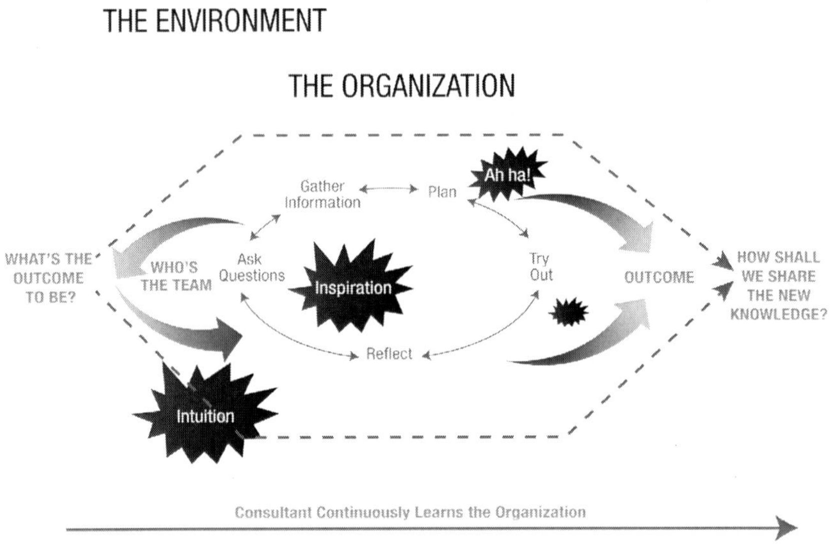

Figure 2.1 An inquiry model of consulting. Copyright Ann K. Brooks and Kathy Edwards

Regardless of the model of consulting we use, the work of consultants is one of changing systems, both human and technical, whether at the individual, group, organization, community, or national level. Whether the intended outcome is an integrated technology system, a talent development system, more efficient operations, employee engagement, or an integrated system of sustainability, change is at the center.

What distinguishes consulting as inquiry from the "expert technical advisor" or the "process" model is that it (a) focuses on outcome; (b) draws on both the consultant's and the client's knowledge, skills, and talent; (c) engages both clients and consultants in analysis, experiment, and evaluation in order to integrate new knowledge and learning into the organization; and (d) fits the process and outcome to the unique characteristics and needs of the specific client organization (Figure 2.1). The model, like action research and action learning, is not linear. Rather, the process of getting to the outcome circles back on itself as needed, with the goal being to find the best way to implement the outcome in a particular organization or community.

A Model of Consulting as Inquiry

If we're not *just* an expert or helper in our work as consultants, and we're not going into organizations and communities to tell them what we know that will solve their problems, what do we do? And what would it look like? One of Brooks's clients tells this story of their work together:

> The company where I was an officer had just acquired a privately owned and profitable company because we thought technology and market penetration would complement our business. The acquired company had 2500 employees in 48 states, with revenues of just under 200 million.
>
> I assumed the role of president and CEO of the acquired company. My board of directors charged me with integrating this acquired company into our company, a publicly traded company on the NYSE, while increasing its long-term profitability and retaining the intellectual talent, which was a key asset of the new company.
>
> The cultures of the two companies were quite different. The acquiring company was quasi-regulated with a large unionized employee base, which was slow to change. The acquired company was nimble with an employee base that was a mixture of employees who could work from home if they chose or work in an office.
>
> Because the founder had located the company in an area of the country with exceptional recreational opportunities and it was near two major universities from which it drew its talent base, he insisted the corporate office close at noon on Fridays to provide employees a long weekend. These benefits were part of the need to retain the professional work force. The acquired company's corporate headquarters provided an onsite gymnasium, a child development center for employees' children, and a variety of workplace enhancements that were far ahead of their time. Its remotely located employees and sales force enjoyed independence, but also support from the home office.
>
> Without exception the employees of the acquired company felt enormously threatened by the acquisition. They felt they were major contributors to the success of their company and would not be recognized by the new company.
>
> Since I was new in my position, I enlisted the help of a consultant [Brooks]. We decided that the challenge was getting *buy-in from the intellectual talent of both the acquired company and the parent company*. So that was what we agreed to as the consulting outcome. This outcome was both strategic and operational. Getting to it was a multi-layer task that was complex and very important to the company, the employees, and various stakeholders. Then we brainstormed and tried to figure out how to get there.
>
> Most people in the parent company felt that the acquired company was profitable, but the employees were too independent, spoiled and would never survive in "the real" world. In other words, there was a great deal of suspicion and mistrust on both sides.
>
> Our challenges were
>
> 1) to demonstrate to senior management and the board of directors that the acquired company's culture was worth preserving;
> 2) to demonstrate to the employee base of the acquired company that the parent company would "do no harm, and take no prisoners";
> 3) to retain the benefits that were important parts of the acquired company's culture and which employees valued highly.
>
> So we asked the acquired company's employees to self-nominate or nominate someone to work on a strategic vision and detailed plan for their company. The group size was eight, which made the group a real working group. The participants developed all the input and format for the strategic plan during an intense two-day session. They then presented the outputs to fellow

employees in a series of sessions and got their support. Finally, the group that developed the strategic plan presented it to the board of directors of the acquiring company.

The results were that

1) the board accepted and approved their plan, including future funding of capital expenditures;
2) the employees who developed the plan became champions for the integration into the parent company;
3) we retained 84% of the existing workforce—an amazing result, given the mobility of an intellectually based professional workforce;
4) the nonprofessional work force decided not to unionize and to retain the flexibility of their working environment.

This story illustrates each phase of the model, from defining the outcome to sharing the new knowledge. The *way* the phases are carried out, the way the partnership and inquiry are enacted, and the balance between use of consultant and client expertise all depend on context, specifically the client's industry or sector and the degree of complexity in the client's environment. We will refer to this story to illustrate each phase of the model.

The Phases of the Model

Each of the following phases describes how clients and consultants can form a partnership aimed at drawing on all relevant knowledge and information in order to achieve a client's desired outcome.

Phase 1: Clarify Outcome and Negotiate Contract

The question, "*What outcome does this client want?*" focuses not only the inquiry process, but the entire consulting engagement. It's a seemingly simple question to ask, but often a difficult one for clients to answer. By focusing on outcome rather than problems, we agree to stay with our clients through implementation. We cannot just give them a solution. We need to make sure they have what they contracted for by the time we finish. A major critique clients have of consultants is that we bring in new ideas and then leave our clients to implement them.

Most of us are trained to seek out and solve problems, particularly as professionals. We look at people, organizations, and communities and are alert to what we can do to fix their problems. Illness, poverty, ignorance, dysfunction, inefficiency, conflict—fixing these and other problems is the work of professionals. Problems can be never-ending, and once we address one problem, we may create or uncover new problems.

This often leads to scope creep, where work is added beyond the scope of the original agreement. Focusing on outcomes rather than problems asks us to look toward creating a new future rather than repairing the past. Focusing on outcomes also shifts perspective towards seeing what resources and capabilities our clients already have that can be enlisted towards getting to the outcome.

Not just consultants but clients have difficulty thinking in terms of outcomes. As Matt Kouri, president and executive director of Greenlights for Nonprofit Success, explained,

> The client doesn't always know what the outcome is they want. About twenty-five percent of the time the client presents a problem where you have to say that's really not your problem. The issue is over here. Then you have a material shift in the contract. Sometimes people feel like that's padding the contract, but it's really not. It's just shifting focus to what's really going on.[6]

Clients may also name a product or service they believe would solve the problem they see (for example, "we need some team building" or "we need to do strategic planning"). Consultants may also be tempted, even compelled, to just provide these services without looking at "what's really going on." We might also offer a diagnosis that leads to the product or service we usually provide, or we may find ourselves "disguising" advice by asking leading questions like, "Have you tried any conflict resolution interventions?"—knowing that we just happen to be very skilled and knowledgeable about conflict resolution. Sometimes, as consultants, we can be so rigid in the "rightness" of our own expertise that we deny or ignore our clients' realities altogether.

When we start asking questions, we often find that the solution our clients want to buy wouldn't get them to the outcomes they want. It is our job to ask those questions and help our clients formulate their "problem" as an outcome. The task in this phase is both to draw our clients out and to help them be more specific about what *they* want to see come out of this engagement. This focuses them on the future, not on the struggles of the past, and begins the process of mobilizing the resources and talents in their organizations or communities toward achieving the outcome. This in turn generates the energy required to figure out the changes needed and implement them.

Our purpose in this phase is to draw out the knowledge, both explicit and implicit, that clients have about their own organizations or communities and help them to look more broadly and deeply, and in new ways, at what their organizations or communities want to be like when we're done working with them. We need to become "naïve experts": naïve about our clients' situations and experts in our own areas of capability *and* in asking good questions.

For consultants, outcome clarity helps us to think about whether or not we *want* to do the work. Do we think the work is interesting? What are the travel demands? Are the client's expectations realistic? Is the client providing sufficient access to staff time or other resources to make it possible? Is the pay worth the time? We can also think about our own capacity to do the work. Do we have the skills, resources, time, knowledge, and experience to do the work? Is the scope of the work too broad? Do we need to bring in another consultant to help us? And as we mentioned earlier, knowing what outcome our potential client is after gives us a clearer picture of whether or not we think the work is ethically or morally acceptable.

Disappointment, anger, and mutual accusations are often the result of clients and consultants not asking as many questions as we need in order to find out what we do and *can* expect from the other. Who will be responsible for what? How will we gauge success? What is the timeline? What will the costs be? Clear outcomes provide a shared touchstone to which both clients and consultants can return when questions come up.

The written contract delineates the desired outcome, scope of the project, the respective responsibilities of consultants and clients, costs, resources needed, time frame, and deadlines, as well as any other details relevant to the project. An inquiry approach requires clients to be active participants in the consulting process, and this conversation facilitates their consideration of their own organizations' time commitments. A comprehensive contract guards against "scope creep."

In the client's case described above, the client and consultant worked together to define the outcome in early conversations about the board's charge to the client and the respective contexts of the acquiring and the acquired companies. This outcome provided a clear focus and boundary for their work together. Had they focused on problems rather than outcomes, the outcome the client wanted may never have been achieved. For example, the problem could have been defined as "communication problems with acquired company's employees" or "resistance of acquired company's employees to changes." These would have been accurate statements of problems that existed, but they would not have encompassed the complexity of achieving both the strategic and operational charge of the board.

Phase 2: Establishing Our Inquiry Partners

As consultants, we partner with several different people in the organization or community. Our first partners, often called "contact clients,"[7] are the persons with whom we work to clarify outcomes and negotiate contracts. Contact clients usually introduce us to others in the organization or community. The contact client may or may not be the "primary client," the person who owns the issue and pays the bill. Since we are ultimately responsible to our primary clients, making sure they are kept up to date on the project is important. Any reports and final decisions on the project usually go to these clients.

"User clients" are the people who are actually doing the work that will be affected by the consulting project. These clients usually have the most "up close" knowledge about the people, systems, and processes relevant to the outcome. They also have the greatest stake in any changes that are made, and so their participation is crucial to a successful outcome. So is the participation of the "end user" clients, such as customers or the people the organization serves.

All of these clients are stakeholders in the project and anything we do will impact them, so their participation is important. Some of them will become working members of the inquiry team. Others will have information or resources that the inquiry team will need.

In the client's story above, the president/CEO was the contact client, the primary client, and a user client. Additional user clients were the employees of the acquired company and the acquiring company's board of directors. Of course, the list of stakeholders extended beyond these to include stockholders, customers, employees in the acquiring organization, and the industry's union.

The Inquiry Team

The inquiry team is the group of persons with whom we partner most closely to figure out how to produce the outcome. It is a collaborative team. We need to work with our primary client to make sure those with the needed knowledge, resources, and place or position in the organization or community are a part of the team. The conversation is important: while we know what specific skills and knowledge are needed on the team, our client knows the individuals and the context.

Most consulting firms prefer to work together with their clients on teams; they may say, "Give us five of your best and brightest, the ones who are going to be in leadership positions in the organization in the next 25 years, and we'll integrate them into our team." Surprisingly, though, research suggests that higher collective intelligence does not seem to be strongly related to the average or maximum individual intelligence among group members.[8] Instead, collective intelligence appears to be most related to the average social sensitivity among group members, the extent to which they take equal turns in conversation, and the percentage of females in the group.

In addition to considering what contributes to a group's collective intelligence, other questions can help us evaluate whether or not we've assembled a project team that is likely to produce an outcome. We can ask, "Which stakeholder groups need to be represented on the inquiry team?" Stakeholder groups may have specific knowledge, interests, and the ability to support or impede the project. The importance of this may not be apparent until the inquiry is already underway and the missing participant becomes evident. One consultant we interviewed described working with an LGBTQ allies organization on strategic planning and realizing as they were in the midst of a crucial meeting with the staff and board that the only person in the room that was not straight was one of the consultants.

Once we have identified relevant stakeholder groups that should be a part of the team, we need to work with our client to select particular persons to represent each group. The person needs to be someone the stakeholder group respects. Without respect, the stakeholder group may not commit the time and energy to collecting data and providing information, nor experimenting with ideas brought from the inquiry group. They will also be less likely to go along with changes the inquiry group wants to implement.

The persons who represent their stakeholder groups also need to have the ability and willingness to collaborate. Research on what makes collaborative teams effective (or not)[9] suggests that the greater the number of people on a team who don't know anyone else and the greater the diversity, the less likely people are to share knowledge. Similarly, the greater the proportion of highly educated specialists on a team, the more likely the team is to devolve into destructive conflict. The same research suggests that both a clear task at the beginning—the outcome, in this case—and consultant skill at attending to the relationships on the team once the team gets going will support collaboration in producing new knowledge. The fact that the outcome is clear provides the team members with latitude to figure out how they want to achieve it, which often enables team members to be open to each other's knowledge contributions. Similarly, including on the team some individuals who know each other seems to contribute to success and support knowledge-sharing.

Team members need to know that each has been asked to participate because he or she has an important contribution to make.[10] This helps to transform what could be a competitive environment into a more open one in which the contributions of others are welcomed.

In the client's story above, the team members were self-nominated or nominated by others to work on a strategic vision and plan for their company. This meant that the team members came to the task with energy and commitment. The team included the president/CEO as well. One of the tasks for both the primary client and the consultant in this case was to manage the power differential between the client herself and the other team members in such a way that team members were not inhibited from fully participating.

Phase 3: Finding Out Who Else Can Contribute

Once the inquiry team is in place and working, it may discover that additional knowledge or skills are needed. Most teams in organizations and communities today are fluid; some members may leave the team and others cycle onto it, and several may be called in for something special that they can contribute. This means that the team itself, including the consultant, is always scanning the organization and beyond, or the community, for people who can or want to contribute something.

Being able to make a meaningful contribution binds people to their organizations or communities. For example, research on community involvement in the schools suggests that while parents may be asked to "get involved" by doing clerical work to help out the school staff, the kind of involvement they may actually want is one in which their contribution is more personally meaningful to them.[11] Bearing this out, interviews with Latin American women immigrants in one research study revealed the importance they placed on activities like preparing and bringing food for student events or staff meetings rather than the copying, sorting, and stapling work they were often asked to do as part of parent involvement programs.[12] The more that stakeholders are given information about the project and the more they are invited to make a meaningful contribution to it, the greater their willingness to support it.

In the client's story described at the beginning of this chapter, no additional members cycled onto the team. The original team remained intact, with the president/CEO playing a diminishing role as the work continued. What she brought to her early participation were credibility for the initiative and support for the team members as they assumed increasing responsibility and leadership on the strategic plan.

Phase 4: The Inquiry Cycle

In the inquiry cycle, the team engages in the creative process of constructing new knowledge for the organization. The inquiry cycle is not unlike the experimental method. The difference is that with consulting, the action takes place in an organization or community rather than in a laboratory.

The methodology of "action learning" as a "collaborative inquiry process in which participants work and reflect on real problems with learning partners, producing a tangible outcome while at the same time learning from the experience,"[13] is particularly instructive here. Its focus on task, eschewing of formal expert knowledge as the only path to task completion, and use of insightful questions to achieve breakthroughs, as well as the importance placed on the role of action in developing new knowledge and the need for team members to *want* to learn from others are all instrumental in getting to a successful outcome.[14]

The inquiry cycle here includes four main sub-phases, similar to the ones elaborated by Kurt Lewin[15] and other action researchers. The constantly recurring steps generally boil down to gathering data, planning, acting, and evaluating. Numerous people have rethought and renamed these steps (as we are doing here), but the essence is the same. It is essentially a cycle of experimentation with the intent of coming progressively closer to the outcome we want. The four phases we identify are (1) take stock of what we already know and what we need to find out; (2) gather and analyze data, information, and knowledge; (3) act based on what we found out; and (4) compare the results of our action with the outcome we want.

Decide What We Know and What We Need to Know

Drawing on action learning methodology, problem-solvers (not experts) use questions to find out (a) what information the inquiry group already has about getting to the outcome; (b) what we believe and think others believe about getting there; and (c) what we may be missing and what assumptions we may be making about the problem. The essential difference between what we propose here and action learning is the importance of identifying and focusing on an outcome rather than a problem.

Gather and Analyze Data, Information, and Knowledge

As we move through this process, we discover what we don't know and need to find out to accomplish the outcome. The term *data* as we will use it here refers to discrete facts, and the term *information* signifies data in context.[16] *Knowledge*, although general agreement is lacking on what the term includes, refers to a fluid mix of framed experience, values, contextual information, and expert insight, which provide a framework for evaluating and incorporating new experiences and information. Knowledge can also include wisdom, insight, and intuition. As consultants and clients we draw on whatever is relevant to our goal of achieving the outcome.

Much of the data the inquiry team wants may already exist in the organization and have already been codified. Data may exist as raw numbers or transcripts, or may already have been analyzed, with conclusions drawn, and produced as information. For example, information on employee classifications, salaries, and length of time with the organization probably already exists. Similarly, the organization may have already conducted surveys various aspects of the organization.

Data gathering may also focus on benchmarking other organizations or communities through analyzing their available information such as mission statements, annual reports, programs, activities, and policies. Acquiring additional knowledge might mean drawing on what is known by outside or inside experts, the insights of others who have struggled with similar challenges or goals, and various analyses and perspectives on the organization's or community's context and future. Knowledge, in itself, is predicated on assumptions and presuppositions. Anyone can produce it. Its value is its usefulness, and its usefulness can only be judged by those who intend to use it.

Consultants often come armed with carefully designed and evaluated data gathering instruments. The tragedy is that data are often gathered using these instruments and analyzed, written into a report, and paid for, but not used. The reason is that they are not specific to the outcome and they are not informed by action. The point with inquiry consulting is that all data gathered must inform what the team does to get to the outcome. An employee engagement survey, for example, is useless unless the results inform actions with which the team is experimenting to see whether or not they get the organization or community closer to the outcome.

Take Action

Drawing on everything the inquiry team learns, we decide what action we should take, make whatever plans are necessary for acting, and act. We are, in fact, conducting action experiments. The actions can range from testing the water with stakeholders who may not be a part of the inquiry team to launching a full-scale information management system. Different members of the team might experiment with different aspects of the project. These actions or experiments yield new knowledge and insights about how to get to the outcome.

One caution about this phase of the project is to minimize the risk of the action as much as possible. Pilot projects with one small segment of the organization can be very helpful in testing an action before rolling out an entirely new initiative or program. However, we do have to take action before we can analyze how close we came to the outcome we're after. As Dwight Eisenhower once noted, "Plans are worthless, but planning is everything."[17]

Evaluate Action Results and Compare to Outcome

As changes are implemented, we need to keep track of how well and in what ways our actions have worked (or not). Always bearing in mind the intended outcome, we can focus on three issues: (a) to what extent the change is working, (b) how the change is affecting the organization's stakeholders, and (c) what the unintended consequences of the change may be.

The first of these is often a functional or technical assessment. Are the technical elements of the project in place? The second and third of these are often overlooked. But finding out how the organization's stakeholders are responding to the changes is critical to a project's success. A website for a restaurant in a community in which word-of-mouth recommendations are more important than a website is likely to be technically successful, but unlikely to be successful in influencing customers. Similarly, an online employee management system may be technically flawless, but may anger professionals in the organization who now must take time away from their professional work to interact with a computerized management system.

Any change in an organization is likely to have unintended consequences. Technical changes are often evaluated as a closed system rather than as a part of the human system they are intended to influence. Does the software work? Do the fertilizer and pesticides produce more abundant crops? Does the elimination of employees produce the calculated profits? But a quick search of both popular and scholarly literature reveals unintended consequences from innovations in fields ranging from medicine to information technology to legislation passed to judicial decisions made.

For example, one vice president for a Fortune 500 manufacturing company described the following change. Thinking from within a short-term financial framework, leaders of her company decided to cut the workforce at her site, particularly older workers who cost more. These were replaced with younger workers or with a contract work force. In the short term, labor costs were cut and profits improved. However, in the long term, worker performance declined because the employees who were laid off took with them a wealth of knowledge about the manufacturing process. Even with extensive training of new workers, without the workers who had the experience and knowledge about the processes, and who knew what to do when crises came up and how to access resources, productivity declined.[18] Anticipating unintended consequences requires, more than anything, the ability to think across systems—or, in other words, to get a bird's-eye view of the many interconnected and overlapping systems of an organization.

This evaluative phase is ongoing and enables the inquiry team to adjust as it proceeds. Robert Stake distinguishes between what occurs in the evaluative phase of the inquiry cycle and the final phase of the consulting project this way: "When the cook tastes the soup that's formative; when the guests taste the soup, that's summative."[19] Inquiry is a formative process. When we look at what we've tried and decide that we've achieved our outcome, that's a summative process.

Phase 5: Sharing New Knowledge with the Organization or Community

Typically, consultants write reports on what they've accomplished. Too often those reports collect dust. Above all, they fail to disseminate knowledge and contribute to learning in the larger organization or community. However, if we think of knowledge and learning as a social phenomenon, then sharing or disseminating it needs to be a part of knowledge creation itself.[20] This is where the importance of inquiry team members' relationships and social networks comes into play, as they serve as conduits for the sharing of knowledge throughout the process. Frank Leistner uses the term "knowledge flow" rather than knowledge management to capture this broader holistic understanding of how knowledge can be shared.

One way of thinking about knowledge-sharing is as marketing. Leistner highlights ways to market or distribute new knowledge that we've slightly adapted to inquiry consulting. Marketing must (1) be ongoing, not limited to a big-bang launch; (2) provide regular updates on the project; (3) use internal and external success stories about both the inquiry process and the outcome; and (4) reach people via the places where they usually spend time.

Drawing further on Leistner, giving the project or outcome a clear brand is also important. For this, organizations or communities might seek a designer to contribute. Physical objects like pins or stickers awarded for contributions to the project may be helpful, depending on the culture. Celebrations of important accomplishments help. Too often personal events like birthdays are overlooked, but such celebrations help bind the team, and as the team grows stronger, others begin to notice. Mailing lists are an important means of disseminating knowledge, particularly in the form of short facts, pictures, and tips for practice. Make sure that the project and outcome hold a place on the agenda of training events and workshops or meetings. The organization's or community's website, newspaper, radio station, and news program are also ways of sharing knowledge. Important to remember, according to Leistner, is that the sharing or marketing of knowledge must appeal to issues that people face. Be consistent in the language used to refer to the project or initiative. The creativity of the inquiry team makes it a good place to generate these ideas. It is important not to depend on a single dissemination mode or event, but to keep people's interest alive by regular dissemination through the channels that are most effective in that particular organization.

In the story above, the data gathering and analysis did not formally go outside of the two-day strategic planning workshop. The team members drew on their own knowledge of their organization and colleagues to develop their vision and plan. However, the inquiry cycle also includes action or implementation. So the team, as the client described, "presented the outputs to fellow employees in a series of sessions and got their support. Finally, the group that developed the strategic plan presented it to the board of directors of the acquiring company." At this point, the group communicated with the president/CEO as it worked to secure colleagues' support, prepare for the presentation to the board, and make the board presentation.

The crowning achievement of this working group was to compare the outcome that had been established for the project with the actual project results. As the president/CEO summarized above, the board accepted and approved their plan, including future funding of capital expenditures; the employees who developed the plan became champions for the integration into the parent company; the acquired company retained 84% of the existing workforce; and the nonprofessional work force retained the flexibility of their working environment. The project was implemented, the outcome was achieved, and the engagement of the team and many of the stakeholders meant that the results were shared across the organization.

The inquiry cycle—indeed, the entire model—is adaptable. As the president/CEO's story illustrates, the phases of the cycle may repeat as many times as necessary; they need not take place in order, nor always be included. The model itself may double back on itself as the consultant and the project team renegotiate the outcome with the contracting client as more information is gathered and the challenges become clearer. The two-dimensional representation of the model is a limited representation of what occurs in the real world.

Getting to Outcome

When consultants negotiate and contract to achieve an outcome together with our clients, we are agreeing to travel with them on an adventure. Like any team of adventurers, we come to depend on each other to contribute whatever we can to optimize our chances of reaching our goal. Inquiry consulting begins with a clear, shared goal. Through a process of inquiry and action, we engage in a shared process of learning in order to move closer and closer to the outcome we want. Those most suited to this adventure are able to share what they know and recognize the value in what others know in a goal-oriented process of experimentation, creativity, and analysis. The result is predictable: a successful outcome. The adventure lies in how we get there. The next chapter looks at what personal qualities consultants need to bring to partnering in inquiry with clients to reach the outcomes they want.

3

The Consultant's Stance

Yesterday is history, tomorrow is a mystery, today is our gift, and we better use it wisely.[1]

—Grandmother Agnes, *Grandmothers Counsel the World*

No matter how many tools and processes we have at our disposal or how much knowledge we bring, the person we've become is our most important resource as consultants. As professionals who work at the interface between knowledge and human systems, how we approach and work with both knowledge and people is central to how effective we are. Drawing on the experiences of successful consultants and recent research, this section focuses on the stance of "not knowing" and its underlying virtue of humility. Then we look at the skill of mindfulness, both as it has developed in the East and in the West. Both are useful to consultants in addressing the ambiguity and unpredictability we face in our organizations, communities, and the world at large. We suggest that to facilitate inquiry and co-create new knowledge, the personal qualities that are needed are not innate, but can be developed.

The Stance of Not Knowing

There's a kind of psychological need to start with a willingness to give up your own stuff—whether accessing your ignorance or being willing to change toward how the client sees things.[2]

—Edgar Schein, Humility and Ignorance: What It Takes to Be an Effective Process Consultant

Engaging in inquiry with clients begins with a personal acceptance of "not knowing," which leads us to openness towards others and the world.

But not knowing is a counterintuitive state for most of us. We feel our clients expect us to know—that's why they've hired us. Our credibility as professionals depends on us knowing how to solve their problems. Better to cling to knowing, even if we aren't sure we do know—and then if they don't implement our advice, it's not our fault.

To not know is also difficult for us because our way of making sense of the world is something we have crafted over a lifetime of experiences and relationships. We defend our understandings of the world because we believe they have worked for us and imagine they work the same for everyone. How we make sense of our clients and their worlds is the product of our own history of learning how to get along in our families, schools, communities, and workplaces. Our sense of who we are is based on the sense we have made of our life experiences so far. If we are independent consultants, we *are* the knowledge and experience we bring. If we work for a consulting firm, we are likely to hold our employment by this or that company as a part of our work identity; failing to effectively deliver our firm's knowledge can feel like failing at our work.

To not know also signals a lack of control. We cannot plan our actions, nor can we rely on "doing the right thing" if we don't have plan. Instead we must rely on others and our own skills in the moment to figure out how to achieve the outcome. For many, this is a frightening thought.

Edgar Schein tells a story of "giving up" in a consulting engagement with executives at Digital Equipment:

> I tried to get the senior management group to behave in a semi-civilized fashion, while they were shouting and interrupting and climbing all over each other. I found that they were very appreciative of my efforts, but it didn't make a damn bit of difference. I finally gave up and it had the feeling of giving up; this was a very important point. When I gave up, my eyes and ears cleared a little bit. I began to try to experience why they were behaving this way. They were not crazy. There was something going on that I just hadn't been seeing. I finally saw that these very smart people who were used to debating with each other were fighting a life-and-death battle and that this was their normal behavior. I saw that my intervention might help them process the information rather than trying to change their behavior. I went to the flip chart and started to write things down, which became a truly helpful intervention because they were losing information. All I did was to enter their process and see what they needed within that process . . . there's a kind of psychological need to start with the willingness to give up your own stuff. . . .[3]

As Schein's story suggests, a very practical reason exists for "giving up." If we are intent on implementing our own agenda (as Schein was at first), then we are only working with half the agenda we need.

Most of us (as in Schein's story) only give up when we don't see any other alternatives. When we finally do let go, we are usually at a loss and unwillingly relinquish psychological control of the situation. We have to be quiet because we don't know what to say or do. In that space of our own silence, we slowly begin to see and understand our clients' (or colleague's, or child's, or partner's, or friend's) world as they do. When we give up in the way Edgar Schein describes it, we stop trying to figure things out and control them. Our minds become open to others and their ways of knowing and acting in the world.

The virtue or strength of character that enables us to truly hear others' knowledge and perspectives and allows us to not know is humility.

The Practice of Humility

> *Humility is the most difficult of all virtues to achieve; nothing dies harder than the desire to think well of oneself.*[4]
>
> —*T. S. Eliot, Shakespeare and the Stoicism of Seneca*

When consultants have inquiry rather than advice-giving in mind, humility is the virtue that enables us to "not know." A virtue is a "pervasive trait of character that allows one to fit into a particular society, even to excel in it."[5] The meaning of the virtue of humility has been different in different moments in history or social spaces.

Most major religions speak to the importance of humility as a spiritual principle. Rather than seeing humility in relationship to God, modern Western psychologists generally view it as growing out of how we perceive ourselves. Thus, in this context, humility refers to "a realistic assessment of one's own contribution and the recognition of the contribution of others, along with the luck and good fortune that made one's own success possible."[6] To elaborate:

> For humble people, there should be no press toward self-importance and no burning need to see—or present—themselves as being better than they actually are. . . . They should also not be particularly interested in dominating others in order to receive entitlements or to elevate their own status . . . [nor should they] magnify their weaknesses . . . while overlooking strengths and successes.[7]

Others have linked humility to a focus on others rather than our own success.[8] What do humble leaders do that distinguishes them from others? One study identified 13 characteristics, based on an academic and business press literature review that focused on stories that identified explicit behaviors of humble leaders. A humble leader

- is open to new paradigms;
- is eager to learn from others;
- acknowledges his or her own limitations and mistakes, and attempts to correct them;
- accepts failure with pragmatism;
- asks for advice;
- develops others;
- has a genuine desire to serve;
- respects others;
- shares honors and recognition with collaborators;
- accepts success with simplicity;
- is not narcissistic and repels adulation;
- avoids self-complacency;
- is frugal.[9]

These characteristics of humble leaders might apply equally to humble consultants.

The theoretical literature also suggests some key features of humility that can help consultants:

- an accurate (not underestimated) sense of one's abilities and achievements;
- the ability to acknowledge one's mistakes, imperfections, gaps in knowledge, and limitations (often with reference to a "higher power");
- openness to new ideas, contradictory information, and advice;
- keeping one's abilities and accomplishments in perspective;
- relatively low focus on the self or an ability to "forget the self";
- appreciation of the value of all things, as well as the many different ways that people and things can contribute to our world.[10]

Most to the point, perhaps, is this: "True humility is more like self-forgetfulness. . . . It leaves people free to esteem their special talents and, with the same honesty, to esteem their neighbor's. Both the neighbor's talents and one's own are recognized as gifts and, like one's height, are not fit subjects for either inordinate pride or self-deprecation."[11]

Nevertheless, we all have a pervasive drive to be better and feel better than the average. In Western social science, many link this drive to maintaining self-esteem. According to one view, self-esteem is defined as "a sense of personal value that is obtained by believing (a) in the validity of one's cultural worldview and (b) that one is living up to the standards that are part of that worldview. It is the feeling that one is a valuable contributor to a meaningful universe—a sense that one's life has both meaning and value."[12] Another view says that self-esteem reflects our inclusion or fitness for inclusion in social groups.[13]

A more postmodern view has introduced the idea of "epistemological humility." Writing about the challenges of the global flow of information without respect for boundaries or cultural or religious differences, Charles Ess notes, "[Epistemological humility is] the understanding that one's best beliefs and views may be *limited*, e.g., dependent upon a specific context, tradition, etc., for their meaning, rather than necessarily shared as universal truths by all peoples."[14]

Even though Ess is writing in the context of the Internet in the 21st century, others have written about the same idea before. For example, Robert Greenleaf's writings on servant leadership linked humility to knowing and not knowing:

> If there is one "right view," which we will generally see as our own, we have no space for the possibility that a different point of view may be valid. Because of that, we have no empathy for those with different views. Because of that, of course, we have no humility. How can we have humility if we've got the answer?[15]

Developing Humility

The cultivation of personal humility is at the center of many religious traditions. Through the Buddhist practice of meditation, meditators cultivate the discipline to more accurately know themselves and the world. Most of us desire whatever we believe will satisfy the illusions we have about ourselves and deny or push away whatever doesn't fit. If we see ourselves as "successful," then we may think we need to drive a European sports car or own a house in the right neighborhood. Humility in this Eastern tradition is seeing ourselves and our surroundings as they are, without illusion.

Some Western psychologists have asked whether cultivating humility is even possible, and concluded that "for individuals to become more humble or modest, they need to override tendencies to inflate their self-images."[16] This sounds similar to the Buddhist tradition. However, in the Western secular tradition, preferred strategies are receiving accurate feedback, transcending self or placing a spiritual entity or other people before self, and becoming more willing to lower our self-evaluation, although little research exists to support the effectiveness of these strategies.

Another approach to developing humility is the use of techniques, resources, or relationships that give people a feeling of security that does not completely hinge on their self-evaluations. Religion, secure attachments to parents or other close relationships, and the unconditional positive regard of significant others in our lives may help. Role models who can themselves accept both positive and negative feedback without overreacting may also help. The point of any of these strategies is to help people feel safe enough to not become too defensive to recognize both the strengths and limitations of themselves and others.[17] Close relationships may also help in that when we are with friends rather than strangers or people we don't trust, our self-serving bias is reduced,[18] and we are more likely to present ourselves more modestly.[19]

Mindfulness

Not knowing is hard. So is humility. To be able to maintain a stance of not knowing requires more than just deciding one day to not know. When our worlds are filled with ambiguity, stress, an overload of information, and others' demands on us, for example, it is difficult to find the peace or the clarity to maintain our balance without propping ourselves up with the things we know and on which we believe we can count. Both Eastern and Western traditions have elaborated the concept of mindfulness. Mindfulness in Western psychology has been conceptualized as the process of drawing novel distinctions. Regardless of how significant or minor the distinction, what is important is that it is new to the person. Mindfulness, in this sense, situates us in the present and enhances our awareness of the contexts and the perspectives we've taken on our current actions; mindfulness can interrupt our habitual and taken-for-granted ways of thinking and acting.

When we are in a state of mindlessness, on the other hand, rules, habits, and routines control our behavior. The novel distinctions that mindfulness can enable us to see can lead us to have (a) more sensitivity to our environment, (b) greater receptivity to new information, (c) new ways or categories for perceiving, and (d) greater awareness of multiple perspectives during problem-solving.[20] Subjectively speaking, one who is mindful feels heightened involvement, wakefulness, or a sense of being in the present.

Mindfulness has been shown to have positive effects in several areas of a person's life. Elderly persons perceive themselves as having more control, which reduces stress and improves health.[21] In business, researchers have found associations between mindfulness and increased creativity and decreased burnout, and in Korea, between mindfulness and increased productivity.[22] Similarly, because people in a mindful state are more present, they are more likely to be perceived as more genuine.

Mindfulness with regard to learning can be encouraged through introducing information in a conditional rather than absolute way ("could be" rather than "is"). Other researchers have shown that when people are told to notice "what is new," their attention improves, as well as their appreciation for the task and better memory.[23] Making information personally meaningful and perspective-taking (for example, looking at a decision from the perspective of each stakeholder) also seems to improve learning. These findings are important for us as consultants to be aware of as we work with clients, since as consultants we are not only interested in knowledge, but in helping our clients with change. We wish to engage them in the knowledge creation and learning that will lead to the process of understanding their worlds differently, taking needed actions, and finally, achieving the outcome.

The concept of mindfulness has also existed for centuries in the East. In the Eastern traditions, mindfulness, or *sati* in Pali, the language in which Buddhist psychology or philosophy was first written, refers to "being able to remember" or "keeping something in mind."[24] For mindful consultants, it is our ability to remember the things we are trying to do to help our clients. For example, if I am trying to co-create knowledge with my clients, I may decide that I want to start listening to them more rather than falling back on old habits and giving them advice. Or, taking a hint from Langer's research, I may decide that I will not offer my own thoughts as categorical fact, but rather as something for us both to consider. Mindfulness in the Buddhist sense is the personal capacity to remember to pay attention to what is going on in the present moment, rather than mindlessly falling back on old habits. Awareness, a companion of mindfulness, refers to the acuity with which we sense or know what is around and within us. We might, for example, be mindful and aware that rather than listening to our client wholeheartedly, we are actually planning what we are going to say next. Mindfulness is noticing that we are not "with" our client, but "with" our own thoughts. Awareness is using our senses to better grasp our clients and their worlds.

As we meditate, we can watch our minds leaping from distraction to distraction, holding onto experiences as if they were permanent, and functioning in a state of near-constant restlessness and dissatisfaction. We see how the perceptions and beliefs we cling to cloud our ability to see situations clearly and are our attempt to make an impermanent world feel permanent. Vipassana meditation, for example, is the practice of "experiencing one's own reality by the systematic and dispassionate observation within oneself of the ever-changing mind-matter phenomenon manifesting itself as sensations."[25] It is the cultivation of mindfulness through meditation in the Buddhist tradition. As our minds clear of our desires and aversions and our emotions calm, we are able to "see" more clearly. For example, one meditator, a businessman, notes,

> [Vipassana] . . . allows me to deal effectively with tensions which arise in my day to day work, enables me to get unstressed quickly, helps me to stay more balanced and assists me to deal with issues with greater insight. . . . I have a greater understanding of cause and effect and most of the time I am able to examine my own motives and reactions without those reactions spilling uncontrollably onto others. I think I am more compassionate—towards myself as well as others—and I am also able to take firm action and speak openly and truthfully. I believe I promote the conduct of the organization's business in an ethical and principled manner.[26]

Both Western and Eastern traditions of mindfulness have ways to train our minds to greater awareness of the world around us, as research increasingly tells us.[27] However, as Karl Weick and Ted Putnam argue, our current account of mind in organizational studies is too weak and will not lead to improved organizational functioning. The weakness is a narrowness that overlooks "preconceptual moments, virtue, concentration, and mindfulness as ways to further develop the mind to control attention and actions."[28]

Compassion

Some consultants and academics believe consultant success relates to self-esteem. Alan Weiss, the president of Summit Consulting Group in Rhode Island, links consultant self-esteem with marketing. In an interview with *Bloomberg Businessweek* he said, "I used to think that most consultants were undercapitalized and that was their big problem. What I know now is that the main problem is self-esteem. . . . They're obsequious and they come to the job hat in hand. If you want to make six figures, you can't have that mindset."[29] However, research suggests that rather than self-esteem, self-compassion may provide the psychological benefits of motivation to productive behavior, protection against the debilitating effects of self-judgment such as depression and anxiety, clarity and accuracy of self-appraisals, and the ability to cope with stress. Self-esteem, on the other hand, has been associated with egoistic illusions about self and failures at self-regulation.[30]

We develop our own capacity for compassion when we can acknowledge our own emotions—pain, fear, joy, pride—and see them in the lives of those around us. We develop it when we acknowledge and recognize these feelings in others and don't avoid or separate ourselves from them. Instead we feel kindly toward them and want to help them. Rather than judging them, we feel as though we understand their suffering. As consultants, when we see one of our clients or a member of a client team "resisting," we can recognize the fear they may be feeling about how the changes on which we are working will affect them or those they care about. The changes we are trying to help an organization or community make may very well be zero-sum games for some members or groups.

Having compassion for our clients is the obverse of having compassion for ourselves. Self-compassion means being open to our own pain and fear and not avoiding or disconnecting from it.[31] We can recognize that the suffering we feel is the same suffering others feel. As consultants, this means that when clients seem to sabotage changes we are helping to implement, at some level they may be fearing that the new world will be different and maybe less desirable to them than the one they are in. As consultants, if we allow ourselves to become aware of our feelings, we may feel anxious that the project or change we are responsible for successfully implementing may fail. Both the so-called resisting client and the consultant may think we are "right" and the other is "wrong." We may each believe that if the other person's ideas about what the organization or community should become are implemented, our own safety or livelihood would be threatened. On a deeper level, figuratively speaking, we may see the loss of solid grounding in the world as a kind of death for ourselves.

Part of what makes it hard for consultants to see others' lives and feelings with compassion, and to also lack compassion for our own weaknesses, is that consulting is a profession that constantly requires us to market ourselves and our services or products. It takes perseverance and is often very competitive. We know we need to stay on the cutting edge of change, we need to present ourselves as experts, we need to succeed, and we need to present an image that conveys we will be successful at what we are being paid to do.

When we are not conscious of our own uncomfortable thoughts and feelings, we are less in touch with what's happening around us. This makes us more likely to stick with what we know, to not really hear what our clients are telling us, and to become rigid about what we do.

While the idea of compassion is usually linked to Buddhist thought, psychology has usefully drawn on what has come to be called "Buddhist psychology" to inform and broaden Western psychology's understanding of the human mind and behavior. Compassion, as a construct in Western psychology, includes (a) "self-kindness," or bringing kindness and understanding to ourselves rather than self-criticism and stern judgment; (b) seeing our own experience as part of the greater human condition rather than as unique and isolating; and (c) mindfulness or keeping our painful thoughts and feelings balanced without over-identifying with them.[32]

Integrity

> *No man is an island, entire of itself; every man is a piece of the continent, a part of the main; if a clod be washed away by the sea, Europe is the less, as well as if a promontory were, as well as if a manor of thy friend's or of thine own were; any man's death diminishes me, because I am involved in mankind, and therefore never send to know for whom the bell tolls; it tolls for thee.*[33]
>
> —*John Donne, The Works of John Donne—Volume III*

It has become a cliché to point out that we live in an interconnected world. When the cliché becomes a concrete realization, we start to analyze the effects of our choices, both as individuals and as groups, organizations, and nations, on others—as well as the effects of their actions on us. The World Health Organization published a paper in 2008 pointing out that these disparities are not natural, but are underpinned by public policy choices and the way social institutions operate. Drawing on the analyses of Klinenberg[34] and of Dreier,[35] the author writes,

> In 1995, a heat wave resulted in the deaths of more than 500 people in Chicago, United States of America (USA). Eric Klinenberg's "social autopsy" of this episode points out that "the processes through which Chicagoans lost their lives followed the entrenched logic of social and spatial divisions that governs the metropolis." People in Chicago's poorest neighborhoods, also with some of the highest proportions of African-Americans as the result of a history of racial segregation, were least likely to have, or be able to afford, air conditioning. In particular, realistic fear of crime kept the elderly socially isolated and barricaded into their homes, while a downsized city government failed to link residents with services that could have saved their lives. In 2005, the impact of hurricane Katrina on New Orleans brought to worldwide attention the deadly mix of racial and economic segregation, failure to invest in adequate flood-control measures despite ample warnings, and the presumption that everyone could afford to get in a car and drive to safety. When the storm hit, those who did not have this option, overwhelmingly poor and African-American, were effectively abandoned as refugees in their own country.[36]

The author's reference to public policy and social institutions suggests that "someone else" is responsible for the deaths of these citizens. And any one of us might justifiably say, "I didn't do that. I wouldn't have done that." But each of us, every day, makes decisions that affect the lives of others and ultimately, our own lives.

The idea of business creating shared value with communities and society suggests recognition of this interconnectedness. However, rather than being based on a moral ethos of "do unto others," Porter and Kramer, who first introduced the idea of "creating shared value," are adamant, as are many of the companies that adopt shared value strategies, that creating shared value is first and foremost, a business strategy: ". . .shared value . . . recognizes that societal needs, not just conventional economic needs, define markets. It also recognizes that social harms frequently create internal costs for firms. . ."[37]

Linking the ire the authors believe people and policy makers direct toward companies' "outdated approach to value creation," they point out,

> [Companies] continue to view value creation narrowly, optimizing short-term financial performance in a bubble while missing the most important customer needs and ignoring the broader influences that determine their longer-term success. *How else could companies overlook the well-being of their customers, the depletion of natural resources vital to their businesses, the viability of key suppliers, or the economic distress of the communities in which they produce and sell? How else could companies think that simply shifting activities to locations with ever lower wages was a sustainable "solution" to competitive challenges?* (Italics added)[38]

For consultants, our first ethical choice (or business choice, if we see ourselves as interconnected with our clients and their communities and the environment) comes when we agree to work toward a particular outcome as we negotiate our contract. We are agreeing to help deliver an outcome. Will our outcome put people out of work? Divert a region's water supply? Bankrupt a company? If we are vague about the outcome, we can overlook or rationalize the effects, both direct and collateral, of what we agree to do.

Appreciating the Gifts and Contributions of Our Clients

One of the most profound shifts in the last 20 years in how we approach change in organizations and communities has been the move from a deficit to a strengths approach. For organizations, David Cooperrider, who began developing the approach based on his dissertation work at Case Western University in 1986, pioneered the shift.[39] For communities, John Kretzman and John McKnight at the Asset-Based Community Development Institute at Northwestern University have elaborated and clearly articulated the importance of focusing on the gifts and contributions members bring. Even consultant guru Peter Block has shifted toward focusing on the importance of assets to building communities and organizations.[40]

In consulting, the use of the term "diagnosis" captures the sense that organizations and communities need healing, usually from the outside in, drawing on the expertise of various professionals who can both diagnose and prescribe a way to fix them. To focus on and highlight the contributions members of organizations and communities can make not only builds the capacity of those individuals to use and develop their strengths, but enlists them in building the capacity of organizations and communities. And importantly, using resources that are already available saves money.

Both those who have contributed to the methods of appreciative inquiry and assets-based community development have developed a variety of readily and freely available techniques and instruments for identifying and engaging people's strengths in organizations and communities. Not surprisingly, both methods begin with inquiry. Both draw on the knowledge and resources of the people present and the extensive networks they are a part of, which extend far beyond their organizations and communities. As consultants, we can always look to ourselves, our consultant firm, or to outside sources for knowledge, expertise, and resources. But we strengthen the capacity of our organization and community clients to make the changes they need to get to the outcomes they want when we look to our clients for the contributions they can and want to make first.

Conclusion

The stance we take when going into an organization or community can set the tone of the relationship. We may bring abundant knowledge or experience with us, and indeed, our clients care that we know what we are doing. But whether and how we are able to use that knowledge, and the kinds of relationships we form with our clients, begin with what we think our work is, what we think of our clients, and how we intend to be and act toward them. This is what we bring to our work as consultants.

Part II

Inquiry into Relationship

We have no basis for consulting without knowledge and the ability to inquire and learn, but neither expert knowledge nor quick and incisive analytic ability will get us to a successful consulting outcome by itself. Clients, for one, may have had little experience with consultants or with "this particular" consultant: "[T]he client may have only a vague idea of how consultants work and may be slightly suspicious—possibly he or she has heard about consultants who try to complicate every issue, require more information than they really need, ask for more time in order to justify longer assignments, and charge exorbitant fees."[1] Similarly, consultants depend on clients to assign qualified managers with whom to work, provide data, and work with them on implementation and the human dynamics of change: "[W]ithout consultant-client collaboration, there is no effective consulting."[2]

Achieving the trust and respect to form a collaborative client-consultant partnership is difficult enough in contexts with which we are familiar. But it becomes even more difficult when times are uncertain and consultants and clients increasingly work with diverse groups of people and in communities, organizations, nations where we encounter beliefs and customs that are different from ours and that we may not understand very well.

Chapter 4, "Emotional Inquiry," explores the role that both clients' and consultants' emotions play in consulting. Beginning with the case of a multimillion-dollar consulting contract in which emotions went very publicly awry, the chapter goes on to see what consultants can learn from neuroscience. Drawing on this research, we identify emotional skills we can use to foster our relationships with our clients and the relationships within our clients' organizations and communities.

Chapter 5, "Partners in Inquiry," looks at the dynamics of collaboration and the kind of trust needed to collaborate in the process of inquiry to create new knowledge. Recognizing the risk inherent in being open to knowledge and perspectives that may not be the ones in which we are invested, this chapter addresses the elements that are central to building, maintaining, and repairing relationships in consulting.

Chapter 6, "Consulting in a Transcultural and Transnational World," goes straight to the challenges of working together when we may not share or even understand our clients' beliefs or the ways they have learned to do things. It looks at how our assumptions about how people, organizations, and communities work can stymie not only our own sense of competence, but the extent to which we can help our clients. We then look at what we can do to make ourselves more effective at working in contexts that, at least for us, may seem very ambiguous and perplexing.

4

Emotional Inquiry

I've learned that people will forget what you said, people will forget what you did, but people will never forget how you made them feel.

—Maya Angelou[1]

The consulting process is tailor made to arouse strong emotions in its participants. The uncertainty about how to achieve an outcome in a limited amount of time, the constant threat of failure, the pressure to make good decisions quickly, and the stress of the changes a consulting project can create all evoke strong emotions. In addition, the need to develop trust swiftly with people we barely know, to work in an environment in which fundamental changes are taking place, and to face the inevitable conflicts and time-consuming nature of working together can all take an emotional toll. It could easily make one wonder why anyone would ever want to be a consultant. Fortunately, the emotional rewards of actually achieving successful outcomes, such as enthusiasm, satisfaction, and joy, are high.

What are some of the consultant's and the client's most common feelings during a consulting project?

Hope. At the beginning of a consulting relationship, both clients and consultants hope that the consultant can help and that the project will succeed. That hope provides the energy to initiate the consulting engagement. Consultants hope our work will be respected. We hope we can help the organization achieve a successful outcome. We want to keep our contract and maybe get another, and be recommended to other possible clients. If we are working for a consulting company, we want our input to be valued and to be given more opportunities and responsibilities. We would like to be promoted. Clients hope that the consultant and other members of the organization will respect their work and value their input. They hope the consultant "gets" their organization or community and can help them get where they want to go. Clients also hope their work on the project results in rewards, either professionally or for the organization or community.

Doubt. Most consultants go into consulting projects wondering whether or not we will be able to help our client. We might also wonder if our client is competent and capable of committing to change. Clients surely wonder the same thing about us. Clients may feel trepidation at bringing in a consultant. Is this consultant competent? Will the consultant just make a bigger mess of things?

Fear. Peter Block observes that most clients experience a fear of losing control and a sense of vulnerability when engaging a consultant.[2] Client stakeholder groups may be wondering what changes might be in the offing. As consultants, we know that we are not in control—the client is. That in itself can cause anxiety. Both clients and consultants harbor some anxiety that we may fail, that others may be critical of our work, or that we might even risk losing our jobs.

Frustration and anger. Inevitably, there will be times when clients feel that we, as outsider consultants, just don't get it, and we're not being helpful. For example, if we miss deadlines or don't return phone calls, clients feel angry and frustrated. As consultants, we may harbor exactly the same feelings about our clients.

Satisfaction. Satisfaction and pride come from success, for both clients and consultants. Such success can mean achieving the outcomes we are working toward, but it can also mean knowing that we have been understood, that our contribution is valuable, and that we have formed or deepened relationships. We feel good when an important insight is shared or when a sense of excitement and hope grows out of the project.

In her book *I'm Sorry I Broke Your Company*, based on her years as a management consultant, Karen Phelan pokes a hole in the myth that people can be managed like machines:

> We have been led to believe by management gurus and management consultancies that businesses are logical and run by the numbers and that their models and theories will provide step-by-step instructions on how to succeed. Companies try to implement these models or make decisions strictly by the numbers and never realize the expected successes because businesses are not actually rational. . . . Businesses are people—irrational, emotional, unpredictable, creative, oddly gifted, and sometimes ingenious people who don't operate according to the theories.[3]

Emotions (and thinking) are natural parts of being human. We expand our skills and abilities to help our clients by honing our awareness of our own emotions, our clients' and colleagues' emotions, and the emotional dialogue we create between us. With little awareness and a lack of knowledge, consulting projects can go terribly wrong.

A Failed Partnership

When we fear emotions getting out of control we tend to respond by ignoring or denying the emotions floating around. When we do not attend to emotions is when they have the most potential to catch us off guard, cause problems in our relationships, and sabotage our projects. We impoverish our work by *not* learning more about emotions—our own and our clients'. They can make or break a consulting project, and the stakes can be huge, as an IBM contract to consolidate data systems for the State of Texas illustrates (Box 4.1).

Box 4.1 A failed partnership

Austin Still Mired in Utility Billing Issues, Blames IBM
Email Exchanges Obtained by Statesmen Show Frustration Was Mutual
By Mark Toohey
Friday, July 20, 2012

Nine months after it was supposed to be finished and running smoothly, the City of Austin's utility billing system is still experiencing million-dollar problems that city officials blame on an IBM staff that has not finished the project.

In a four-month string of increasingly frustrated emails to IBM officials, obtained by the American-Statesman through an open records request, city officials paint a picture of missed deadlines, broken promises and general shoddiness on the company's part.

Those higher-ups respond that IBM is working diligently to correct the problems, some of which the company said the city also bears responsibility for fixing. . . .

Utility executives say that between the billing system's problems and the additional staffing, Austin has lost more than $8 million at last count.

"I understand for a multibillion dollar (company) that may not be a significant loss, but to the citizens of Austin and our small $1 billion (electric utility), these losses are very significant," Alan Claypool, Austin Energy's chief information officer, wrote in a mid-June email to Julie Romero, director of energy and utilities for IBM Global Application Services.

A month later, Claypool wrote to Bridget van Kralingen, an IBM senior vice president: "We have grave concerns this passive-aggressive culture . . . is prevalent in the IBM operations and the City of Austin will continue to suffer financial losses as a result."

Romero wrote in response that Austin Energy misunderstood conversations between its employees and IBM's and that the city shares some of the responsibility. Van Kralingen later added in an email to Claypool: "Thank you for your note. I understand . . . that our team is working through the situation with your team."

> Those exchanges came months after IBM and the State of Texas parted ways over an $863 million project to merge the data centers of 28 state agencies into two upgraded and streamlined facilities. The state had been trying to fire the company, and in March, the two basically split the tab to walk away from the failed project. . . .
>
> From *The Austin American Statesman*

Anger, resentment, accusations. Like a bad divorce, the project's failure hurt not only the two organizations, but also the employees of both groups and the citizens who paid for and expected to be served by the two agencies.

Emotions such as these affect more than just our immediate client and us. Other stakeholders in the project, even though we have no direct contact with them, may react to what we do. The IBM case illustrates this. In spite of the apparent "technical" nature of the project, emotions splashed beyond the consultants and clients immediately engaged in the work to the larger consulting organization and to citizens and civic leaders in the community. Ignoring emotions can carry a high price tag, both in terms of the immediate contract and our reputation. They can also provide valuable information for consultants as to the effectiveness of our work. A project may be technically perfect, but in terms of human systems, a disaster. Emotions are one of the key "data points" we have in understanding the human context of our work.

Were there clues? What might the clients and consultants have picked up that could have warned that this project was "going south?"

Fear of Feelings

Neither IBM nor the City of Austin behaved any "worse" than most of us. We often *under*-attend to emotions in our work as consultants, in large part because we are so focused on our own expertise and using it to help our clients. Part of our lack of focus on emotions may also be the long-standing bias against emotion in the workplace in many cultures. This is true in the U.S., for example. Being emotional in the workplace in the United States has conventionally been feared as potentially "out-of-control" behavior, as harmful to relationships, and as irrational and therefore detrimental to sound decision-making. As Fineman points out, "In many management circles, it is a cliché to assert that 'emotions shouldn't cloud your judgment.'"[4]

Similarly, the consultant literature pays little attention to emotions. Echoing attitudes in management circles, Lundberg and Young[5] write about consultants, "It is as if feelings are taboo and cognitions the only legitimate currency of discourse. . . ." Thus, it is no wonder that many of us "don't see" emotions, either in ourselves, or among our clients. Instead, we may recognize we are angry or anxious, but fight back those feelings in order to present a calm and rational presence to our clients and colleagues. Or we may glide over our clients' obvious emotions, changing the subject or pushing our agenda harder. For many of us, the presence of something that seems unpredictable, overwhelming, and potentially beyond our skill set to manage impels us to stay rational when emotions threaten to escape.

Emotions as Data

Emotions, however, are important data for consultants, although usually when we think about data, we think about the "hard facts." Only recently has science begun to look at emotion as an important dimension of human functioning, and both neuroscientists and behavioral researchers are learning a lot that can be useful to consultants.

Our own emotions can be an excellent gauge of what is going on in relation to our clients. For example, if we feel inspired and energized by an organization's leader, the chances are that other people do, too. By the same token, if in a conversation with a manager, we end up feeling put down and stupid, it will come as no surprise to find that many of that manager's direct reports experience that person in much the same way. Or there will be times when something is happening in the organization that just doesn't "feel" right to us. That is our cue to keep inquiring and exploring the source of that feeling.

These "feelings" seem to arise from our brain structures and circuits and can range from being so subtle as to be barely noticeable, to extremely painful, for example when we feel humiliated or threatened, to wonderfully pleasurable, like when we are successful at securing an important contract or are celebrated for an accomplishment. Arguably, these emotion-generated feelings have contributed to the thoughts and actions that lead us to achieve the goals we set for ourselves.[6]

What Science Can Tell Us

Scientists have been working to increase our understanding of emotions for decades. Some of their findings are particularly helpful to consultants.

Emotion and Cognition Are Linked

That how we think and how we feel are interwoven in ways we don't even recognize is only dawning in historically rational and technologically accomplished cultures and nations:

> A fundamental characteristic of Western science and philosophy is the conception of the thinker as alone rather than embedded within a human community. It is a philosophy that leads us to look for answers that are technical and abstract instead of looking within lived experiences and human interactions. (Cozolino, 2006, 10)[7]

Whether or not we believe we can separate our emotions from our thoughts, scientific research demonstrates that the two are integrated. Emotions, moods, feelings about our own thinking (difficulty recalling or "feeing foggy" and so forth), and bodily sensations all can influence our judgments.[8] Researchers have found that moods can influence not only inconsequential decisions, but also very important decisions such as medical school admissions[9] or stock market investments.[10]

In one study carried out during the immediate aftermath of the September 11, 2001 terrorist attacks on the World Trade Center in New York, researchers induced persons to focus on the fear they experienced. When focused on fear, they increased their assessment of their risk and enhanced their plans to take precautionary behavior. On the other hand, when researchers induced persons to focus on their anger, their assessment of risk and plans to take precautions decreased.[11] Drawing on these two examples as consultants, we might make wiser decisions and act more competently if we take note of our mood when we make judgments about potential clients or assess the riskiness of a particular intervention or project.

Research also tells us that particular emotions affect our financial decisions. Sadness elicits a desire to change whatever our current state is, resulting in reduced selling and inflated buying prices. Disgust triggers us to purge or acquire less, with the opposite effect on our willingness to pay, even when the emotions we are feeling were the result of a previous and irrelevant situation.[12]

Neuroscience has enabled us to see ways in which feeling and thought are intertwined. Using MRI technology, researchers have been able to watch our brains at work. For example, scientists have seen the emotional parts of the brain "light up" rather than either the "cold" reasoning or the emotion-regulating parts of the brain when strong supporters of candidates are asked to make reasoned judgments about information that threatened their own or the opposing candidate during the 2004 U.S. presidential campaign.[13] We can call reasoning that is influenced by emotion "hot reasoning." We might well wonder which parts of our "consultant brains" light up when we receive and need to evaluate information that is threatening to or supportive of the success of a project on which we're working. Which parts of our clients' brains light up when they hear the same information?

Emotion and Change

Since consultants are in the business of change, what can science tell us about how emotions may play into the change process? Whether we are implementing a new software system, coaching or developing a team, or helping with strategic planning, we are intervening in the status quo and fomenting change. Even if we are conducting training or fact-finding, or evaluating a program, the ultimate intent of our work is to change something for the better. Nothing in organizations is more emotion-laden than a change process.

The often-used term *client resistance* refers to our clients' understandable opposition to having their worlds reordered in ways that seem out of their control and often counter to their well-being. Research suggests that negative emotions in response to the experience of ongoing change in organizations are linked to perceptions that the future is insecure, working conditions will be inadequate, and treatment by the organization will be inadequate. The result is likely to be a loss of employee trust and employee withdrawal.[14]

Srinivasan S. Pillay, a neuroscientist and psychiatrist, offers several insights from neuroscience into why change is such a challenge to the human brain.[15] For change to occur, the action center (motor cortex) of the brain has to be activated. The brain has to process "forces 'for' and 'against' change."[16] "Most people recognize that for change to occur they have to think about a situation," Pillay writes. "But many people also leave out the feeling or emotion when they are trying to change. If they do this, the brain's accountant is missing vital information. When there is resistance to change, it is very rarely a missing thought process. Most often, it is a missing emotion."[17]

He also observes, "We tend to increase the value of our choices after we make them." The brain's reward center is activated in favor of the choice we have made versus the ones we rejected. Also, "when we have a challenging emotional task, the brain will shut down."[18] And finally, conditioning makes it more likely that our brain prefers to continue with the habits and patterns it has already formed. So it is no wonder that it is difficult for people to change a path once they are on it. Pillay recommends making small decisions to help move us in the direction of the change we are trying to make.

Our knowledge of emotion and neuroscience can help us both to not be blindsided by reactions to change and to be sure to include emotion in our planning implementation of change projects. Change does not happen automatically or easily in the human brain and consequently neither in our clients nor in ourselves. Understanding the naturalness of the emotions we feel when faced with change, particularly when the particular change is at the discretion of someone else, can provide us with a more insightful understanding of "client resistance."

Emotions Are Shared

Emotions are contagious. Individual moods and emotions affect group moods and emotions and vice versa.[19] We can pick up the hope, excitement, and pride as well as the fear and anxiety, hopelessness, and anger of our clients. Similarly, they can pick up our emotions and those of each other. All humans have "the tendency to automatically mimic and synchronize facial expressions, vocalizations, postures, and movements with those of another person and, consequently, to converge emotionally."[20] Emotions are a little like a virus. They are hard to vaccinate against or manage, but awareness of how we "catch" them in our relationships can make us better consultants.

Emotions are passed from one to another through two basic processes: mimicry and feedback. We seem to automatically mimic or synchronize the way we talk, hold ourselves, make facial expressions, and move in accord with those around us. For example, in some cultures in Asia, people smile or laugh when they are embarrassed or angry. Many neuroscientists have observed that certain parts of the brain are activated when we see others act and that this enables us to plan our own and understand others' actions. Other researchers have noted that monkeys communicate their fear to others through face, sounds, and posture and that these serve as a warning to other monkeys of possible trouble.

What can we learn from this research? First, we know that humans, both men and women, are using all of their senses as well as what others say to figure out how a person or a group is feeling. As we process information about others, we also learn how their emotions affect us.

We can also see how easily consultants and clients alike can get sucked into letting negative emotion drag us down. Especially in an organization in distress, emotions may be very intense and very negative. When we let the bad mood of a client or organization rub off on us or take us over, we have lost our usefulness to our clients.

How Can Emotions Make Us Better Consultants?

A noted economist, Jonathan Cohen, argues that humans are *unable* to act in accordance with their long-term goals (maximization of utility). This challenges standard economic theory. He adds that various behavioral economists suggest that we do not act in our own interest because we have (a) limited information, (b) limited ability to learn, (c) limited ability to focus and control behavior, *and emotions get in the way*.[21]

Is that what happened to IBM and the City of Austin project described above? We can presume that both parties *wanted* their project to succeed. We might even imagine how the factors cited above contributed to each party acting against its own best interest. Did IBM have enough information about the employees who were supposed to work with the new system? Did the company's expertise get in the way of learning more about its client? If IBM consultants did sabotage their own project, they wouldn't be alone among consultants or humans in general. As one researcher pointed out, "[the fact that] even revered figures, including Catholic priests, celebrity/sports role models, and respected political leaders, have been publicly castigated for their spectacular failures of self-control is a testament to the difficulties inherent in trying to control self."[22] How discouraging for all of us!

Nevertheless, there is hope. Neuroscience suggests that we have an impressive capacity to become more effective in monitoring and regulating our own emotions and relating to the emotions of others; we also have the capacity to use this awareness to become better thinkers and to act in ways that produce better interactions with our clients, thus increasing our chances of getting to the outcomes or results we want.

How can we use this amazing capacity to self-regulate that neuroscience assures us we have? Can we develop this natural ability to help ourselves become more effective consultants and human beings? How might what we are about to say or do embroil us both in an emotional tangle that is counterproductive to the work we're trying to do together? The recognition that our emotions can trigger us to act in destructive ways is, doubtless, at the bottom of the taboo in organizations against bringing our emotions to work.

The fact that we can be aware of our emotions as they arise, and even name them, is a powerful skill and one to be developed and honed. But even if we can see our own anger, frustration, and pride, for example, and name them—and on a good day, even make the decision not to act on them—we may still be left with an emotion smoldering and making us miserable and on the verge of acting in ways we know we might regret. We can also use our ability to self-regulate to direct our attention towards our clients' and colleagues' emotions and become more aware and knowledgeable about them—about how they feel about us or the project, for example, and about the dynamics at work in the organization.

So what next? We can recognize an emotion, and we can name it. What can we do so that it doesn't dominate our day or sabotage our work? The amazing human capacity to self-regulate means that in the split second before we react, we are also able to self-regulate our behavior and then choose whether to say or do what we may feel impelled to say or do. Admittedly, this can be difficult to do because the energy of the emotion is still with us. This energy is likely why the taboo on emotion in the workplace exists. If we can't manage the emotional energy, then it's best to forbid it.

We often take our emotions with us, whether we acknowledge them or not. For example, we may have started the day feeling angry or out of sorts, or had an argument with our partner or housemate. Then we leave for work, taking that emotion with us, even though we try to shake free from it. If we commute by car, we find ourselves getting angry at the person who just cut in front of us or at the line of traffic we're stuck in. We react aggressively, racing and cutting ahead of the car in the lane next to us, or we honk. We get to work and find ourselves irritated by those around us, or we get angry at our computer or our desk chair or the pen that just ran out of ink and no one ordered more of the kind of pen we always write with and now we have to use some stupid pen that gets ink all over our fingers. Grrrr!

What we have done when we fail to observe and acknowledge these things, when we mindlessly take the emotion into each new situation or interaction, is to start an internal dialogue with ourselves about how and why this new situation or interaction makes us angry. The anger stays. The lines we say to ourselves (or others) changes with the context, whether it's anger at our partner for expecting something of us we can't do, anger at traffic or people for cutting in on us, anger at work about the things that aren't the way we want them.

We don't have to do these things. When we recognize our emotion—say, anger—we can diffuse it by going for a walk, taking a shower, seeing a movie, going to the gym, or doing a little yoga.

We can also make our emotions the focus of our inquiry. We can use our analytic abilities to look at the emotion. Where did it come from? What kinds of things am I thinking or doing as I take this emotion with me into the day? How is this emotion affecting me? How is it affecting my ability to think? How is it affecting the way I stand, walk, or move? What effect am I having on other people or on the climate of my workplace, my colleagues, or my client?

Emotional Skills

We can become skillful with emotions (a) by paying attention (to our own emotions and the other person's, as well as to what's going on between us); (b) by empathizing; and (c) through curiosity (Figure 4.1). All of these lead to increased honesty and trust among stakeholders to a consulting project. Each of these have been researched by both neural and behavioral psychologists, and whether we are conscious of our own capacity in these areas or not, as humans, we have capability in all of these.

Attention

Consciously or unconsciously, we feel our own emotions. Edgar Schein cautions consultants, "Check out your own emotions and intentions before offering, giving, or receiving help."[23] The extent to which we experience these feelings reflects the extent to which we have learned to "stuff our emotions". When we stuff our emotions, we cut off one very important source of data about ourselves and our clients.

Attention or being mindful of what is going on with us enables us to become increasingly conscious of our own emotions and so better able to make decisions about whether or not we will act on them. If we are too busy "stuffing" our own emotions, how we act or what we say is more likely to be a raw reaction, without thought—a verbal punch. Or we may simply block out what is going on emotionally for both our clients and ourselves, in an effort to push our agenda through. This is most likely

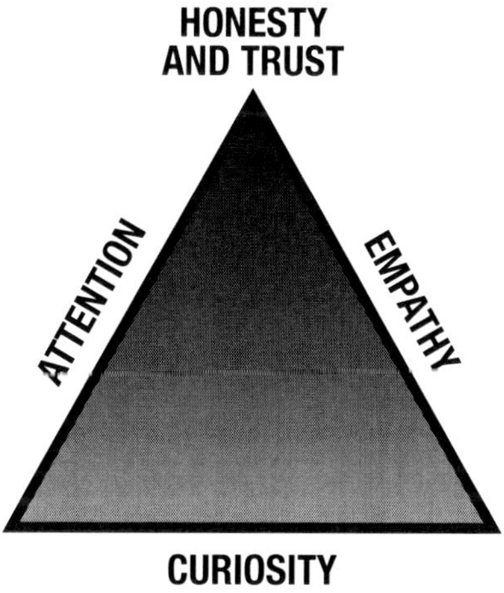

Figure 4.1 Elements of emotional skillfulness

to happen for consultants when we have a plan or a methodology or a package we intend to use to solve our client's problem and are either overwhelmed, threatened, or just plain unwilling to enter into the swampy unknown of doing something else. Research over the last decade shows physicians and patients are highly reactive to each other's emotions, as indicated by increased heart rate and skin conductance.[24]

Sometimes, we are simply so self-absorbed or absorbed in details of our own work that those around us fail to penetrate our awareness. In *I'm Sorry I Broke Your Company*,[25] Karen Phelan tells the story of a "problem employee," Frank, who was part of an on-site consultant team tasked with benchmarking various financial measures with their client's competitors. When the team met, he was missing because, as it turned out, he lost track of time as he sought out the information. The next day, when the team presented its findings to the project leader, the young consultant distributed printouts of his spreadsheets, comprised of rows upon rows of data. He then enthusiastically began to explain each number. As Phelan describes it,

> After about three minutes of details on financial numbers, the project leader shouted, "Stop." Still enthusiastic, Frank asked, "Do you have a question?" "Yes," was the reply, "What the hell is this?" . . . The whole room burst out laughing. When we all settled down, the project leader shook his head and asked for the next presenter. Frank was crestfallen and humiliated. He also seemed a bit bewildered, and I felt bad for him.[26]

We can imagine how badly Frank wanted to succeed. He was sure his success rested on his technical expertise. He seemed completely unaware of the people and emotions around him.

But the stakes tied to becoming more aware of and reflective on and capable of regulating our emotions are not just our own humiliation, as in Frank's story, or our general emotional misery and suffering—the stakes are also our ability to think.[27] When our emotional reactions are of such intensity that they go beyond our window of tolerance, our behavior and thinking can become disrupted. At such times, cognitive functions like abstract thinking, self-reflection, and metacognition or thinking about the effectiveness of our own thinking shut down, and we become incapable of rational thought. Physically, we may experience an increase in heart rate and respiration or a pounding in the head, a sense of numbness, or muscle tension.

The better we are at paying attention, the more acutely we become aware of the small moment between feeling an emotion and acting on it. Surprisingly, Frank's humiliation drove him to not join his consulting team for dinner so that he could make his numbers even better and redeem his poor performance. Repeatedly, he interacted with other consultants and clients as though he were emotionally tone deaf. Finally, when their comments during his presentations about his detailed explanations of the minute details of his data in meetings became increasingly loud and mocking, he seemed to get it. According to Phelan, he turned to the room of people and said, "I get it. You don't think this is interesting and really don't care. You probably just want to know the highlights."[28]

Many of the emotions we feel in consulting grow out of our relationships with others. What are our clients thinking and feeling? How are they reacting to us or each other? We are seldom neutral observers of either our own or others' emotions. Instead, we are carefully reading faces, body language, tone of voice, language, and context to infer others' emotions. Without both paying attention to what we are learning about them and catching the split second before we react, we most often, do, in fact, react.

We have the innate capacity to be vigilant about others' positive and negative perceptions regarding us and what we want. If we feel threatened or supported regarding what we want, we are likely to react. If we can stop, for just a moment, we can take stock of what is going on emotionally in ourselves and with our clients or colleagues. We can then choose whether what we are about to say or do will, in fact, contribute to our work together or create confusion, defensiveness, hostility, or embarrassment. Often the best choice is, as Edgar Schein pointed out, to stop and wait. Don't do or say anything. This allows space for the work to emerge in a way that fits our client's world better and maintains a working and productive client-consultant relationship. We may feel "out of control" for the moment, but in silence rests the possibility for context-specific creativity and innovation.

Empathy

As important as honing our skill to pay attention to our clients' emotions is using our capacity to empathize with them. Empathy refers to being aware of and sensitive to, and vicariously experiencing, the feelings, thoughts, or experiences of others without them having to explicitly explain them to us.

Empathy points us toward the "space between"—or where we interact, verbally or not, with each other. This is not something we have to "get." This is the "sharing [of] others' internal states and explicitly considering those states" that neuroscientists have identified as an apparently innate human capacity.[29] It is a "prosocial" mental process and our skill at empathy depends on how concerned we are about the well-being of others.[30]

In other words, the extent to which we are skilled at empathy depends on our choice to be skilled. It is up to us! Further studies suggest we can improve our abilities (neuroplasticity) and that they can be developed through training and practice in the same way humans can practice to improve musical performance. To demonstrate this, one researcher sent physicians through a series of training modules designed to improve doctor empathy. The training was designed to help them become better at recognizing patients' nonverbal cues and facial expressions. It also helped them with ways to deal with their own physical responses to highly emotional interactions and situations. Those who went through the training maintained better eye contact, interrupted patients less, and maintained their equanimity better when patients became angry.[31]

Like doctors, as consultants, empathy makes us better at what we do. Physicians with greater empathy have been associated with happier doctors, fewer malpractice claims, more satisfied patients, better patient outcomes, and fewer medical errors.[32] The value of empathy extends to business as well. One strategy consultant examined why Microsoft succeeded so admirably with the Xbox, cornering the video game system market, yet failed so miserably to compete with the Apple iPod in the portable music player market with their Zune product. He quotes one member of the Microsoft development team: "The biggest challenge with Zune was trying to figure out who we were building it for. With Xbox, we knew those guys. Hell, we were those guys."[33]

Certainly, our empathy for those we see as "like us" may come more naturally. But in consulting, our clients are not always "someone like me." We may find it hard to empathize with an employee in our client's organization or community who seems to be resisting (there's that word again) or actively destroying what we're trying to create. How can we succeed with the project if "these people" keep getting in our way? But we can also develop our empathetic capacities through shifting our perspective from "me" to "them" and managing our own emotional upheavals or reacting rather than pausing before we act. Neuroscience has shown that meditation can increase this capacity. Gathering more information about our clients can also help us.

We can also "let go" of our own narrative of what success means and open up to other possibilities. In Phelan's story about Frank earlier in this chapter, we can witness how he let go of his own success narrative, which centered on technical expertise with financial analysis, to finally recognize that his clients' narrative of success was considerably different. But our own narratives are compelling. We are the heroes of these narratives. All others are peripheral players.

This becomes obvious when we look at the difference between how consultants and clients define performance success. "Me" is central to each of their performance indicators (Table 4.1).

If we can move from being engulfed in narratives centered on our own success, however we may define it, and shift our attention to the experiences and feelings of our clients, we can often begin to build an understanding and solutions that are very different from and even exceed our own carefully planned and tenaciously held view of what is and should be happening. We might even become partners!

Curiosity

Curiosity is central to both attention and to empathy. As noted earlier, the human capacity to be curious is innate and has neural correlates. When we are embedded in "me," we lack curiosity. We stop gathering information. We stop trying to understand. Little wonder that the NASA spacecraft sent to explore Mars was named the Curiosity Rover. Curiosity is at the heart of inquiry and is the center of the approach to consulting described in this book. It is what helps us to navigate the uncertainty that has always characterized human life.

Table 4.1 Comparison of client and consultant perspectives on indicators of consultant performance

Top performance indicators identified by clients	*Top performance indicators identified by consultants*
1. Achieving agreed-upon objectives	1. Customer satisfaction
2. Customer/client satisfaction	2. Profitability
3. Timeliness of service delivery	3. Repeat business
4. Recommendations actually implemented	4. Personal/job satisfaction
5. Achieving measurable results	5. Referrals
6. Delivery within forecasted budget	6. Revenue
7. Regular updates during engagement	7. Growth
8. Provision of post-engagement support	8. Meeting the budget (8 & 9 equal)
	9. Longevity of consulting practice
	10. Number of clients/size of client base

Based on Alan Simon and Vanya Kumar, "Clients' Views on Strategic Capabilities Which Lead to Management Consulting Success," *Management Decision* 39, no. 5 (2001): 362–372.

The Big Payoff: Honesty and Trust

> It is a mistake to assume that clients make decisions to begin projects and use consultants based on purely rational reasons. More often than not, the client's primary question is: "Is this consultant someone I can trust? Is this someone I can trust not to hurt me, not to con me—someone who can both help solve the organizational or technical problems I have and, at the same time, be considerate of my position and person?" When I operate in too clever or manipulative a way, or lay it on too thick, clients pick this up. They are thinking to themselves, *Wow! This guy is really laying it on thick. He is making me look like a fool if I say no.* Line managers know when we are trying to maneuver them, and when it happens, they trust us a little less."[34]

The trust we extend to others, neurologically speaking, seems to involve the very same brain structures as do emotions.[35] Although the research has not linked trust to specific emotions, fear, suspicion, and anxiety don't appear to be bad guesses.

Trust speaks to the quality of our relationship, so it is little wonder it figures so prominently in the literature written for consultants. To build trust, Block recommends authenticity or putting into words for our clients what we are experiencing. Assuming that he means putting into words those parts of our experience that would be helpful to our client, he is asking for consultants to be reflectively self-aware of our emotions as they come and go and to be skilled at self-regulating our expression of them. Not all that comes into our minds is helpful if it comes out of our mouth. The skill of being authentic with our experience (at least with ourselves), yet skillful in deciding how to express it and when to share it is a skill to be practiced.

Schein gives examples of intentions that suggest we are not ready to help another, such as "getting the job done" or "beating someone in a game."[36] Aggressive intentions like these, which are not uncommon in the workplace and among consultants and clients alike, carry with them emotions like frustration or anger. Such intentions and emotions are sure to fray, if not destroy, trust. Before acting on such intentions or emotions, pausing and observing ourselves and our clients can give us the space to reconsider our intentions. Are we in it for ourselves? Are we in it for them? Are we in it for both ourselves and our clients? And even a step beyond that, are we also in it for the larger organization, community, or world?

A Breach of Trust: Exploitation of Emotion

Given our capacity to regulate our own emotions, gather information about those of others (including scientific information about emotions), and then alter our own behavior accordingly, we are capable of doing immense good as well as taking negative advantage of others through using our emotional skill. The field of marketing and its sub-field of "neuromarketing," which is based on neuroscience research documenting the effects of biology on decision-making, have been particularly skilled at drawing on neuroscience research methods to influence consumers and voters.

Management scholar Stephen Fineman points out the danger that emotions can be used by organizations for power or oppression: "Emotions such as love, fear, anger, fury, resentment, embarrassment, happiness, joy, envy, and sadness appear as tradable social resources or commodities; something that can be negotiated, manipulated or pushed aside; engineered by cultural patterning or managerial prerogative; subtly steered or perverted in social encounters; bought and sold."[37] Even though we usually think of emotion as very individual and biologically based, social norms can shape what we come to see as acceptable in the emotional realm. He uses the example of how business has utilized the feelings of pride and commitment and conflict with competitors to shape an economic war narrative.

The corporate world has institutionalized such sentiments in its philosophy of marketplace wars and battles, so much so that one management consultant describes it as

> a battle cry drilled into the skull of every employee, from top to bottom. In casting competitors as enemies, it follows that they can be derided and "crushed," and their defeat celebrated. Conversely, losing a battle is to be attended by feelings of humiliation and resentment—and then aggression to fuel a further round in the competitive "war."[38]

Conclusion: The Power of "We"

Emotions. Ignoring them doesn't make them go away, it just makes us stupid about them. Suppressing them is a blunt tool when used with emotions. It simply shuts down our inquiry into what's going on with our client and leads us to unskilled interactions with our clients.

Understanding and becoming skillful with emotions contributes to trust between clients and consultants. The building blocks for transforming what often seems to inherently be a relationship of mutual self-focusedness and lack of trust are attention, empathy, and curiosity. They are the innate riches of human beings. Neuroscience tells us we can allow them to atrophy, or we can train them. They move us beyond "me" and "you" to "us" or a partnership and the possibility of creating something new and innovative, something better able to respond to the challenges and changes of our uncertain world.

The next chapter addresses client-consultant relationships.

5
Partners in Inquiry

According to the computer consultants that I studied, technical aspects were less crucial for the success of projects than the social relations within project groups and in relationship to clients. . . .

—Alvesson (2001, 874)[1]

We live in a world that is often characterized as filled with conflict, materialism, and blatant self-interest. And we work in a profession that is frequently caricatured as the most money-grubbing and manipulative in the world. Even the most positive stereotypes of consultants focus on concepts like leveraging intellectual capital, becoming thought leaders, and utilizing analytics.

But consulting is really about relationships, and client-consultant relationships are one of the most complex around. They both intrigue and perplex researchers and writers. By their nature, they are usually temporary, while at the same time marked by intensity and even urgency. The stakes may be high, emotions volatile, and the pressures enormous. But these relationships can also be some of the most exciting and energizing relationships we ever engage in because for this moment in time, an organization or community has opened itself to the possibility of learning and change.

Typically, the consultant-client relationship is thought of as two parties interacting: "me," the consultant, interacting with "you," the client. Phrases like "consultant influence" and "client resistance" are common. This perspective on relationship functions well in a predictable world. In an uncertain world where a more open and inquiring stance is needed, a different understanding of the consultant-client relationship is needed, too.

What if we shift our thinking from "me, the consultant" and "you, the client" to "we"? What if we think of the space we occupy during the time we work together as one we create together? What are we each bringing to that space that can be used to make the project successful? How are we each contributing to the quality of that space? Is it a space that is open enough to welcome all knowledge and perspectives? Is it a space that is forgiving enough to enable creative combination and recombination of the different knowledge each of us brings until we come up with a way forward, which draws on all available expertise and fits the specific context? We are challenged, whether we take up the challenge or not, to take account of "we" and the space we occupy together. What kind of space will we make together? Developing and sustaining "we" relationships takes both the heart and the head.

The "Win-Win" of "We"

Thinking of the consulting relationship as "we" can result in outcomes greater than either "you" or "I" could have come up with alone. Lynne Gilfillan, who has led scientific and technical consulting firms for over 30 years, tells about her experience trying to create a collaborative consortium in the pharmaceutical field:[2]

> The business of developing drugs to treat really scary diseases like Ebola is incredibly difficult. Not only are there very large scientific and technical hurdles to overcome, but there are non-trivial business issues, and entrenched interests as well. One of my clients believed that only by combining the best of the intellectual talent, physical resources, business processes, and social milieu of big pharmaceutical companies, federal laboratories, small biotech companies, and academic research laboratories would there be enough critical mass for the enterprise to succeed. I immediately saw the potential benefits of collaboration and became passionate about the project as well.
>
> Unfortunately, these organizations were frequently "at war," battling over the market space and federal funding. They had relationships, because each had at least one thing the others wanted and didn't have, but they were more used to working in boss-underling relationships than in more equal-to-equal collaborative relationships. There was a serious lack of trust. Finally, none of them believed that the collaborative team we were proposing had any chance of succeeding, and the pharmaceutical industry is sometimes characterized as being very traditional and resistant to change.
>
> So, we brought several leaders, scientists and managers, in for an initial visit, one organization at a time. The first thing was listening to what each organization thought was special and unique about itself. It was fun for me and for them, too. After all who doesn't like to talk about themselves to an appreciative audience? We asked lots of questions, and it was obvious to each organization that we were really interested in learning about them. A bonus for me was that I learned a lot about some really innovative science.
>
> Only after we had heard what they had to say did we talk about the collaborative organization we were trying to form. And then we asked them how we could make the new organization better. In every instance but one, we heard really good suggestions for revisions to our original approach. We heard a lot of doubts too, but in most cases the organizations had good suggestions to resolve the obstacles they saw. And although the organizations, without exception,

> entered these initial meetings with the mindset that they were wasting time, all but one ended the meeting by signing a Memorandum of Understanding to be a member of our organization.
>
> Given that we had believed we would be lucky to get 20%, we considered ourselves to be very fortunate. The result was a team 104 organizations strong, built to attack the development of therapeutics for deadly infectious diseases like Ebola.

A partnership that invites the knowledge and experience of all parties to the table asks us to consider that none of us knows all there is to know in addressing a challenge. In fact, as this story demonstrates, what we can accomplish when we relax enough to make space for the knowledge of others is bigger and more innovative than any one of us could have come up with alone.

This is a very different relationship than the more traditional one, where the consultant comes in and attempts to solve a problem by imposing an installation of some kind on the client. This relationship is based on the consultant knowing more than the client; Schein refers to it as a "one upness" dynamic that places clients in a subordinate role.[3]

Most of us would be much more comfortable and safe recreating the world in our own image. We feel more in control. But the downside of this approach can be disastrous, as illustrated in this second story from Gilfillan:

> I have a colleague whom I work with infrequently, and whom I would not characterize as collaborative. He is a very, very smart guy, who knows a lot about the pharmaceutical industry. His specialty is helping organizations write proposals. On the last proposal on which we consulted, he never even bothered to ask the client about the scientific or organizational approach that they wanted to take for the proposal. He started the first meeting by telling them what they should do and how they should do it. He essentially wrote a proposal for them, and not only didn't listen when they told him that much of what he had written was not what they wanted to do, but, when he did bother to listen to them, he told them that their approach was wrong. He talked over people never even giving the impression that he was interested in what they had to say. It was like watching a train wreck in slow motion. The client began to view him as a bully, not surprisingly, and began rejecting everything he provided, even the good stuff. The moral of the story, if you don't really listen to and engage with your clients as full partners, they'll stop listening to and engaging with you as well.

"Train wrecks" like this are a high price to pay for clinging to our own expertise as consultants.

Collaborating as Partners in Consulting

Working together and sharing knowledge to achieve an outcome is often referred to as collaboration. Alan S. Cohen, an expert on networks who has been involved in several successful startups, explains, "[I]n Silicon Valley 'collaboration' is defined as something you do with another colleague or company to achieve greatness—something to be praised—as in: 'They collaborated on that beautiful piece of software.'"[4] Another definition is "the synergistic relationship found when two or more entities working together produce something much greater than the sum of their individual abilities and contribution."[5]

The idea of consultants and clients collaborating is becoming more common in consulting circles. Consultant and author Keith Merron calls such a client-consultant relationship a partnership and writes that it is

> a partnership in which together, the client and the consultants "are touched by each other." Together they create an authentic, vulnerable relationship, where the client, the process, and the relationship itself are all explored, deepened, and enhanced. They see their work together as co-creative and filled with learning that is every bit as imaginative as it is well designed.[6]

Some consulting firms and consultants are moving toward the idea of collaboration and partnering as well. Namisha Kachhla, a new consultant with Capgemini, remembers her first project meeting: "I was really surprised when I walked into the room and I could not tell the difference between the clients and the consultants. Everyone was contributing."[7]

Creating Inquiry Space

What is needed to create the space for clients and consultants to be partners in inquiry? How do we set the conditions for creative collaboration to occur? Asking questions and listening in inquiry, and having the emotional skills to engage in collaboration, are crucial for the creation of space for inquiry to succeed. We think these skills are so important that we have devoted entire chapters to those issues. But other relational issues impact our ability to create and nurture our partnerships in inquiry as well.

Physical Space

Ideally, collaborative space for inquiry includes a quiet, comfortable room with flexible furniture where partners can work for extended blocks of time without interruptions. Access to food, data, media, and other resources are readily available. Samsung, for example, has a process to encourage innovation that the company refers to as "lock 'em up," where participants are isolated together and face a deadline to produce.[8]

In reality, collaborative efforts take place in all sorts of unusual places. In writing this book, for example, we did much of our best thinking in walk and talk sessions around a lake and in a variety of small coffee shops. We've had productive collaborations with clients in elevators, parking lots, restaurants, and cars on the way to the airport. Edwards even recalls one breakthrough in thinking with a client while sitting on the tailgate of a pickup truck in a field.

The point is to actively work to create space where people can be comfortable to be creative together. However, we can and do collaborate anywhere.

Mutual Respect and Caring

Having respect for each other as inquiry partners means believing that each person has something unique and potentially important to contribute. This means valuing others' contributions as much as our own. Since neuroscience has shown us that thinking and emotions are intertwined, respecting others' ideas also means respecting their feelings. Edwards shares this story of the role of feelings rather than rationality in one of her client's decisions:

> I was recently working with a client whose office was located in the historical district of her community. Her lease was ending and it quickly became clear to me that she could save a great deal of money by moving to a less expensive part of the city without much impact on the business. But she adamantly refused to consider such a possibility. She said, "It gives me joy to get up and go to work every morning. I can only feel the culture and history of my community here. Otherwise my business could be in any city anywhere. And I am sick of the Wal-Martization of the world. I would rather not be in business than give up my connection to my community." This may not have been the best financial decision. It also may not have been the choice I would have made. Her decision was obviously more from the heart than the head. I had to respect her feelings, and I admired her values.

Closely related to respect is caring about each other. Caring means wanting the best for our partners. It means wanting them to benefit as much as we do from this consulting engagement. It means wanting to know who they are and being able to work hard and still have fun with each other. It means helping our partners grow and welcoming the opportunity ourselves to grow from the relationship. Consulting can be done without caring, but caring about our client/partners both binds us more tightly to our clients and is the backbone of a consult-client relationship that is more resilient and more moral.

Caring is what shifts consulting from a business transaction to a relationship. Instead of a relationship based on telling, defending, demanding, requiring, influencing, and compelling, a caring relationship incorporates listening, responding sensitively through inclusion and dialogue, and sharing aspirations, joys, and accomplishments.[9] Edgar Schein uses the word "helping" in a similar way: "Obviously, if I have no intention of being helpful and hardworking at it, it is unlike[ly] to lead to a helping relationship. I have found in all human relationship that the intention to be helpful is the best guarantee of a relationship that is rewarding and leads to mutual learning."[10] If we do not care about our clients, we should not consult as a partner in inquiry.

Honest Dialogue

Honesty is at the core of collaborative consulting. In many working relationships, people are afraid to be honest with each other. Unfortunately that fear is well founded in some organizations, where mistakes are punished and firings are common. The fear of speaking up has been around since ancient times. Erik de Haan quotes Euripides, who wrote around 406 BC, as saying, "[F]irst I would learn whether I may speak freely of what is going on there, or if I should trim my words. I fear your hastiness, my lord, your anger, your too potent royalty."[11]

According to Erik de Haan, "fearless speech, being open and honest, without fear of the consequences," is essential to "fearless consulting."[12] Not only do we want to be honest and transparent with our clients, but we have to be just as fearless in welcoming input from them even when it is hard to hear. A free, open dialogue between partners can only enhance inquiry.

However, we do have to be careful to choose our moments to share, especially if what we are sharing is information that can be interpreted negatively. More than one consultant has entered into an organization, community, or nation, for that matter, and proceeded, as an outsider, to tell its members what they were doing wrong. Needless to say, that kind of approach can lead to an early exit. So sensitivity is important. How would we feel if we were receiving the critique? Timing is important, too. Is the moment right? Would our clients come to the same insight if we just gave them a chance?

Openness to Ideas and Collaboration

Collaborative inquiry is not a typical way for most people from the U.S. or many Western European countries to relate to each other. It may be more common in parts of Asia, even while negotiating the nuances of hierarchy. However, in the more individual-oriented society of the U.S., our knee-jerk reaction when someone questions our ideas or has a different one is to get defensive. We may argue or hold on to our own position even more strongly. Particularly if we are in a position of responsibility or authority, we often feel great pressure to have all the answers. Socrates, for example, was great at asking questions, but also put people on the defensive. His lack of skill in that respect may have led to his demise.

For a collaborative inquiry into how to get to a particular outcome partners must be able to ask and to listen to many questions, even when we don't have the answers. We need to become adept at holding steady and continuing our search for what would work best in a space of uncertainty. What keeps this process from turning into chaos is the goal toward which we're headed: What's the outcome we're after?

With this in mind, we foster space for creativity to take place, a protected space in which we can be open to all ideas. But letting go of our tendency to judge is not an easy task. However, as we see that ideas can come from unlikely sources and experience how they build on each other, combining and recombining, and ultimately transforming into something we could never have imagined on our own, we begin to feel safer in letting go of our own most favored thought. This is the creative process of collaboration. Consultants can model collaborative behavior for our clients by not rushing to tell what we know, by asking for and welcoming what others know, by showing our enthusiasm when new ideas emerge, and by seeking what can be appreciated rather than critiqued in another's contribution. Edgar Schein hints at the possibility of such creative vulnerability on the part of consultants when he suggests, "when in doubt, share the problem." He writes,

> I am often in the situation where I do not know what to do next, what kind of intervention would be appropriate. It is often appropriate in those situations to share the problem with the client and involve him or her in deciding what to do next.[13]

Collaborations depend on the ability to be open to each other's ideas and a willingness to build on them together.

Willingness to Take Risks Together

To discover something new we often have to take a risk. The risk may be simply to stop trying to control the process. It may be sharing our own vulnerability. It may be asking questions instead of giving answers. It may be sharing a hard truth. Or it may be depending on our clients' competence.

But taking risks is hard, especially when we feel we must perform. Independent health consultant Linda Donelson described how she grew to become capable of taking risks:

> Consultants have to have enough experience that they are sure of themselves, because it is only when you are sure enough of yourself that you are able to really expose yourself, and to take the risks and the gambles. Because to be a good consultant, sometimes you have to be a little bit foolish, and you can't do that if you are too tight. And maybe I say that because . . . my tendency historically was to be too tight. In a way, that's how consulting is good for me, because it lets me to be more open, and looser, and more relaxed.[14]

Taking risks in our relationships and experimenting with actions are part of the inquiry process. However, if things do not go well and responsibility is to be assigned, we should take it on as consultants. As outsiders, we usually are not nearly as much at risk as our clients inside the organization. By the same token, credit goes to our clients. Recognition can be hard to come by in organizations. And surprisingly, taking responsibility and sharing credit more often than not reflect well on us as consultants. And our reward comes from knowing we helped others succeed.

Challenges for Collaborating Partners

Client-consultant relationships are characterized by several challenges, which require considerable consultant and client skill. Partnering to achieve outcomes requires that we not only begin to concern ourselves with how clients view their world and our performance, but that we become conscious of and skillful at working with the relationships we develop. This is not just noting that "I did this" and "they did that," but how we are both contributing to the way our partnership develops.

Trust

Trust in the consulting relationship has two dimensions: trust between consultant and client and consultants' trust of ourselves.

The most talked about is whether consultants and clients trust each other. The client needs to be able to trust that as consultants we have the client's best interests at heart, will protect the client's confidentiality and proprietary information, will be competent, and will be interpersonally adept. In essence, they want to know that we will "have their back." As consultants, we need to trust our clients to provide the access and information we need, to collaborate as full partners, to not sabotage our efforts, and to be honest with us about what's really going on. Clients and consultants need to trust each other to give honest feedback throughout the project and to work hard to contribute all of our knowledge and talents in the service of achieving the outcome. Maintaining trust can be demanding because large sums of money, jobs, and even the continued existence of the organization are often at stake.

Given that the organization or community and the consultant are often new to each other, we often need to build a foundation of trust immediately. Learning to develop trust quickly with people we do not know well is an important consultant skill.

In one book for consultants directed specifically at the matter of trust, *The Trusted Advisor*, the authors present four elements that engender trust between consultants and clients: credibility, reliability, intimacy, and a low level of self-orientation or focus on oneself.[15] We build credibility by demonstrating our competence and honesty. We are reliable when we do what we say we will do when we say we will do it. Intimacy is about becoming emotionally close. To this last point, research says that the more we know about someone, the better we like them.[16] So by sharing personal information, including—at the right moment—our own vulnerability, we build close relationships with our clients and contribute to a trusting relationship. The element of a low level of self-orientation refers to setting our own self-interest aside. According to the authors, "The most egregious form of self-orientation is, of course, simple selfishness, being 'in it for the money.' However, self-orientation is about much more than greed. It covers anything that keeps us focused on ourselves rather than our client."[17]

In the course of our work as consultants, inevitably we will inadvertently say or do things that hurt another person. No consultant wakes up in the morning and says, "OK, how can I damage a relationship today?" But because of the sensitive and intense nature of consulting relationships, we are bound to bump into other people's feelings. This is where mindfulness or remembering to pay attention comes in. We stay mindful of what is going on between ourselves and our clients so as to recognize when we offend them or when we feel offended and are on the verge of reacting in a way that is likely to damage the trust we are building. We pay attention, not only to "me" and "you," but also to "we," and tend to the space between.

When we need to repair trust, Leigh Thompson suggests practical steps we can take:[18]

- Suggest a personal meeting;
- Put the focus on the relationship;
- Apologies;
- Let them vent;
- Do not get defensive;
- Ask for clarifying information;
- Test your understanding;

- Formulate a plan;
- Think about ways to prevent future problems;
- Do a relationship checkup.

The sooner we take steps to restore trust, the better. When the focus is on "we," most relationships can be repaired. In fact, when we successfully work through an incident of broken trust, the relationship may actually become stronger.

The less discussed dimension of trust is consultant trust of self. Like all professions, consultants starting out grapple with the fear that we don't know enough, won't be able to perform, or will be seen by our clients or colleagues as not doing a good job. Often we feel safer sticking to the formal knowledge we've learned or someone else's published step-by-step plan for how to do whatever we've been asked to do, whether it is a strategic plan, a workshop, or a financial analysis. As we try to figure out how to implement what we've learned, we are so preoccupied that we often lose sight of how we are relating to our clients, the aerial view of the organization or community and how our piece fits in. We are consultants, often with a professional qualification, and perhaps, some related work experience. Someone is paying us for our work, but we don't yet have enough depth of experience to look beyond a fairly rote application of what others have taught us or tell us to do. In that sense, we are still in the early phases of taking on the identity of our profession, either in our chosen area of expertise or as consultants.

Those of us who have more experience and have developed a stronger identity in our profession may, on the other hand, have too much self-trust. We are more likely to assume that what worked in a previous client experience will work with a later client. This faulty generalization means that we tend to ignore the uniqueness of the later client and her context.

Describing the unconscious reasoning that contributes to us assuming that a current situation is like ones we've been in in the past, Daniel Kahneman writes, "the perceptual system and intuitive operations . . . generate *impressions* of the attributes of objects of perception and thought. These impressions are not voluntary and need not be verbally explicit."[19] Considerable evidence exists to support the idea that two distinct systems for processing information are at work in the human brain; one is conscious and deliberative, while the other is unconscious and intuitive. Tacit knowledge,[20] or the knowledge that expert practitioners draw on, is a part of the unconscious and intuitive fund of knowledge we have available. For experienced consultants, intuition "draws on a deep and rich knowledge base from extensive experience within a domain."[21] However, these assumptions may mean we miss seeing the actual reality of the new situation and insist, as did the "train wreck" consultant in the earlier story in this chapter, on our own perspective.

Not all consultants rely equally on the intuition they've developed based on their past experience. According to research, different individuals seem predisposed to rely more on either intuition or deliberation.[22] Additionally, as time pressures increase, we seem to rely more on our intuition than deliberative processing.[23] For experienced consultants, the patterns we've developed to make sense of the challenges our clients face are our richest resources. The risk is that important patterns in one context may be less significant or even irrelevant in another. This risk increases when we work within societies, cultures, and nations with which we have limited familiarity.

The old adage that if we have a hammer everything is a nail is apropos here. Just because we have a background as a psychologist, trainer, engineer, and so forth does not mean that the problems our clients bring are rightly interpreted as needing psychological testing, training, or engineering know-how. Our best protection against our knee-jerk solutions is to be mindful of our cognitive inclinations toward intuitive judgments based on our past experiences.

Psychological Safety

Inquiring together with our clients to achieve an outcome means that except for our shared commitment to the outcome, we are entering the unknown. Of course, we may all feel a little insecure—we like the known and to feel in control. Accordingly, with our clients in inquiry, we must be conscious of their psychological safety. In other words, do those working together on the project believe that it is safe to take risks?[24]

Early research on this issue found that those with a comparative lack of power were hesitant to contribute to the teams they belonged to, which were trying to improve work processes. Those remaining silent had less education, held a lower position in the organization's hierarchy, or were not members of the dominant gender, race, or ethnic group in the organization.[25]

Taking this research further and testing a model of psychological safety, Edmondson found that psychological safety goes beyond interpersonal trust. Rather, there seems to be what she refers to as a "coherent interpersonal climate" with each of the groups in her study that was characterized by some blend of trust, respect for the competence of the others, and caring about the others on the team as people. She quotes the members of one team as saying that they "want to work together to make the product better."[26]

Thus, while trust is important in consulting relationships, so is psychological safety. Consultants set a climate of safety when we work with clients to identify a clear outcome, model a climate of respect for all stakeholders' competence, and demonstrate an attitude of caring about our clients. In this way we can invite in the knowledge of all participants, fostering the space needed to collaborate to produce the new knowledge that is needed.

One Upness

One insidious threat to collaboration is what Schein calls one upness.[27] Consultant power and control are embedded in the assumption of the consultant role as one of expert. This automatically puts clients in a one down position. But it works both ways. Sometimes clients feel the need to maintain power and control and so one up the consultant. This dynamic can lead to an adversarial rather than a collaborative relationship with no chance of partnership or collaboration.

The double sword of defensiveness and aggressiveness that is characteristic of one-up interactions is illustrated in an interaction Mirela Schwarz and Timothy Clark describe from their research:

> At one meeting the partner consultant suggested the client buy a small automotive supplier that would open a new market for the client. The CEO responded quickly, "No, this does not work for us, just forget that immediately . . . that's nonsense . . . couldn't your people come up with something better than this?"[28]

We can hear the door slam on the client and consultant thinking together about what might work. When we try to be right and compete to win to protect ourselves and maintain control, one-upmanship kills collaboration. One way we can disarm such defensiveness as consultants is to pause so as not to react defensively ourselves, setting off a client-consultant war of sorts, and to ask questions to find out more about what our client is thinking. These questions must come from a place of genuinely caring about what our client thinks—they cannot be questions that disguise a one-up reaction.

Our Client's Baby

One of the most difficult tasks for consultants is to not become so invested in the consulting project that we lose sight of the fact that ultimately, our client has to own and live with both the intervention process and the outcome. We may like our own preferred solutions to our clients' challenges too much. Edwards tells a story that shows how easily we can lose sight of this:

> Whenever I am tempted to blame a client for not moving fast enough to change, or "resisting" my brilliant ideas, I am reminded of a story from my own family. My sister's baby was born prematurely, contracted pneumonia, and was placed on a ventilator. Every day for weeks the family and friends kept vigil at the hospital hoping and praying for a miracle.
>
> I particularly remember an older couple from our small hometown, who drove twenty miles to the hospital every morning and stayed every evening until dark. They didn't say much, just sat in supportive silence. Their presence was comforting. After weeks of watching, it became clear to me that the ventilator was all that was keeping the baby alive. I began to urge my sister and her husband to turn off the ventilator. They were not ready to do that.
>
> Finally one day, alone in the waiting room with the elderly couple, the stress got to me and I snapped, crying and ranting that I could not understand how my sister and brother-in-law could choose to prolong the agony of the situation. Our friend broke her silence, turned to me and quietly said, "The baby is dead. She is not going to recover. But it is not your baby. You do not know what you would do in this situation if it was." I instantly recognized the truth of what she said and let go of my judgment about the situation. Ultimately, the baby was declared brain dead, and my family could grieve without the added burden of a heartbreaking decision. But I have never forgotten the life lessons of those words: "It's not your baby."

Senior consultant Tim Garippa reflects on facing a boundary issue that is common for consultants. Telling about his work with a client to develop an interactive training system, he talks about the many people with different expertise who were needed to bring the idea to fruition. He candidly describes his own struggle to let go of control of the project, which he felt had become his "baby":

> Other members beyond the person I was working with came in and began to make decisions. They were making technical choices I didn't think were optimal. For example choosing to use TV instead of rear-projection. I would get visibly upset. My investment had exceeded what was ok. I regret that I didn't take the time to help the client see what I saw. They also brought in a design company to help set up the rooms. The design company got excited about it. But I viewed it as a threat. I considered the project mine.
>
> But if you don't let go of making it yours you won't be successful. The more people who know what you're doing and who share the knowledge transfer the better. The way it was put to me was if we make the client successful, we'll be successful. More work will come our way if we make other people look good. That applies to your fellow consultants as well as clients. It's natural to want to blame somebody when something goes wrong. But it's not productive.[29]

Real people's lives and livelihoods are at stake in every decision that is made. Our stakes as consultants are very different from those of our client organizations, institutions, or communities. James McKinsey, the founder of McKinsey & Company, shared his own insight into this on his deathbed. After temporarily leaving his consulting firm to become chairman of the board of Marshall Field in Chicago, he caught pneumonia and died at the age of 48 after a stressful trip to the company's mill in 1937. As he was dying, he told a friend that it was a lot harder to run a company than it was to consult with one.[30]

We can empathize with our clients; we can even forget that the project and outcome ultimately belong to them. But we can never fully know what "walking in their shoes" feels like. Clients' decisions do, indeed, belong to them. And when we truly become partners in inquiry, the reward is in seeing our client's world become better.

Conclusion

The costs of collaboration can be high. For starters, it can take more time to work together to partner in inquiry than to simply tell our clients what they should do, or do it for them. The apparent simplicity and efficiency and the illusion of control can be like the Sirens singing to Odysseus on his journey home. And in a perfectly predictable situation for which an expert, technical solution is appropriate, a client-consultant partnership to figure out how best to reach the outcome seems like overkill. Partnering and collaborating ask us to engage in more relationship building and monitoring than most of us want to do when we see a goal, think we know how to get there, and just want to get it done!

The challenge is determining which outcome can actually be accomplished in such a straightforward technical manner. A careful look at consulting disasters suggests that we may overestimate the number of problems we can solve with a skilled technical solution. How uncomplicated our work would be if we didn't have to pay attention to relationships and the peculiarities of contexts!

This chapter has been about building and maintaining relationships as consultants. This is challenging enough with people with whom we share a common background and experiences. However, increasingly, we find ourselves working in contexts where different rules, different assumptions, and different languages predominate. The next chapter addresses these challenges for consultants.

6

Consulting in a Transcultural and Transnational World

Nearby, two men, one black and one white, sat together, dressed in identical white thobes. Alan's guidebook told him there was a pronounced, even naked, racism in Saudi Arabia, but here was this. Perhaps not evidence of societal harmony, but still. He could not think of an instance when a custom or dictum described in a guidebook had ever been borne out in practice. Conveying cultural norms was like reporting traffic conditions. By the time you published them they were irrelevant.[1]

—Consultant Alan Clay in Dave Eggers, *A Hologram for the King*

Consultants are increasingly working for organizations in cultures and nations different from our own. Cultural differences add an extra layer of complexity. Working in cultures to which we have not been socialized is like playing a game of Monopoly on a chessboard. We think we know the rules, only to discover we are playing an entirely different game from everybody else.

Consider, for example, an Australian consultant doing an evaluation of a large international aid organization's maternal health improvement project in rural Southeast Asia. Part of the data she gathered came from community focus groups in rural areas. Her evaluation partners were from the same Southeast Asian country. After completing her own focus group, she went to listen in on some of the groups being facilitated by her Southeast Asian colleagues. They had all taken notes on what they believed to be the important points that community members had made. However, when she and her colleagues compared what they had observed and believed was most important to the evaluation, she found that her own list radically differed from her Southeast Asian colleagues' lists, which were very similar to each other. She was struck, she said, by how differently the two nationalities perceived the same event.

Her reflection on this *intercultural* consulting team should give us all pause about assuming that we understand what is "going on here." Our cultural and historical socialization both directs and limits what we look for and see. The only safe assumption is that we all interpret events through the lens of our own cultures and histories, and each one of us may embody multiple cultures and histories reflecting our nationalities, families, ethnicities, education, work experiences, generational cohorts, and community cultures.

Our work as consultants in such contexts requires both inquiry and expertise. On the one hand, we need to learn as much as we can about the cultures and the people with whom we're working. We also need to balance inquiry with expertise, to balance the need to work together with our clients to find new solutions with cultural expectations that we, the consultants, "be" the experts. All of this requires us to be both acute and subtle in our inquiry and adept and flexible in our tactics and interactions.

We are also increasingly working with groups of people who are being referred to as *transnational or transcultural* and claim more than one nation or culture as a part of their identities. This is the case for an increasing number of people worldwide, including consultants. And we are working with *multicultural* organizations and groups comprising people from a variety of cultures and nations or who identify with diverse ethnicities, races, genders, ages, sexualities, and abilities.

This diversity means that we may not clearly understand the interpersonal and group dynamics going on around us, and that our own words and actions may be heard in ways we never imagined. This makes our work both more risky and more complex than it would be if we were working with people who had been socialized in ways similar to us and in organizations with which we are comfortably familiar.

Distinguishing between *intercultural*, *transnational/transcultural*, and *multicultural* environments is important in that they require different knowledge, experience, and skills from consultants. Intercultural here refers to interactions across the boundaries of two or more cultures; for example, when a person from Sweden works for the Ghanian government, both engage in an intercultural relationship. The terms transnational/transcultural here refer to a single entity, such as a person, family, or organization identifying with more than one nation or culture. Finally, multicultural refers to several ethnicities, cultures, or languages interacting within a single organization or nation. We will address each of these separately (although in reality, they often overlap) in this chapter.

Intercultural Consulting

With so many consultants working in cultures outside our comfort zone, interest in transcultural issues is starting to bubble.[2] The structures and practices of management are areas in which we are likely to immediately encounter variations across cultures and nations. Such differences can also exist *within* nations, as many have observed in moving between the East and West coasts of the U.S., the French- and German-speaking parts of Switzerland, Shanghai and Beijing in China, or Sydney and Melbourne in Australia. Some ways in which management practices may vary are how organizations or communities handle age and seniority; the role traditional authorities play; whether they tend toward more democratic or autocratic interactions; whether they are more interested in achieving individual or group success; what groups of people socialize together; the acceptability of offering feedback, appraisals, and criticism; whether "go-betweens" play an important role in influencing people; the meaning of meals and drinking; expectations regarding punctuality and how quickly things get done; and how minorities are viewed.[3]

A wealth of research and practical expertise has accrued in the fields of communications, international development, and international education, as well as in the government sector engaged in international work and international nongovernmental organizations (INGOs). Nevertheless, the mainstream business management literature has been slow to draw on this expertise.[4] An exception is a chapter in Milan Kubr's classic book on management consulting, in which he writes,

> [P]ersonality and value system have been molded by the culture in which he or she has grown up, worked, and socialized. Yet the consultant may be unaware of it. For as "the last thing that fish will discover is water," often culture will be the last thing that a management consultant, otherwise an outstanding expert in a particular technical field, will discover.[5]

Even for those who are seasoned at living or working outside of our own countries, being confronted by things we have long taken for granted is part of the territory when we leave our own "fishbowls."

Countless definitions of culture exist. Geert Hoftstede, a Dutch social psychologist who carried out a pioneering study in IBM on values across nations, defines culture as:

> the collective mental programming of the people in an environment. Culture is not characteristic of individuals; it encompasses a number of people who were conditioned by the same education and life experience. When we speak of the culture of a group, a tribe, a geographical region, a national minority, or a nation, culture refers to the collective mental programming that these people have in common; the programming that is different from that of other groups, tribes, regions, minorities or majorities, or nations.[6]

All of us embody an amalgam of group and cultural identities. Nevertheless, scholars and consultants have found it useful to identify patterns that seem to characterize national cultures or regions of the world. Such cultural patterns can be seen in the folktales, proverbs, and story lines that appear again and again in the literature, films, and art of particular cultures or societies. So, for example, while U.S. literature often portrays individual heroes overcoming difficulties in the external world, Japanese literature delves into the lives of people who are frequently preoccupied with their inner worlds and consciousness. Stories and art with themes like these, the stories we grow up with, socialize us and help us to make sense of our own identities. Knowledge of these national and group characteristics is important for consultants.

One American manager who led a project to design an interface for a Japan-U.S. cross-national customer data system tells of writing an e-mail to her U.S. manager and her Japanese team members pointing out flaws in the system they were building. While her U.S. boss appreciated her directness, her Japanese colleagues saw her as disloyal and treated her accordingly:

> They literally put my office in a storage room, where I had desks stacked from floor to ceiling and I was the only person there. So they totally isolated me, which was a pretty loud signal to me that I was not a part of the inside circle and that they would communicate with me only as needed.[7]

Brooks worked for some years in a large Japanese multinational corporation in Japan. She recalls that while living in one of the large company-owned apartment complexes, she observed apparently misbehaving school-aged children punished by being locked out of the family's apartment, a dramatic socialization into the values of loyalty and conformity. Writing for the international business community, sociologist John Alston and his colleague Issao Takei explain this further:

> Rejection by one's group members is a major form of punishment for a person guilty of nonconformity. Group members expect loyalty and total dedication to the group's goal. On the other hand, the group is expected to take care of loyal individual members. This reciprocity of benefits forges tightly knit groups that are highly productive and efficient. In the past noncomformist members of a village or urban neighborhood were shunned and ostracized by fellow members. This act, called *mura hachibu*, is still found in contemporary Japan including those in office and workplaces. A co-worker who has make [sic] a serious error or shown a lack of loyalty is avoided by his peers; people will even hesitate to sit next to him during a meeting.[8]

Thus, as international consultants, to not understand the "mental programming" of people socialized into the dominant culture within which we are working is not just a matter of etiquette, but one of success or failure. As the experience of the manager above illustrates, our own mental programming means that even with the best of intentions, we are very likely to reap rewards (or punishments) we didn't expect.

Dimensions of National Cultures

Despite the challenges of seeing past our own socialization, we are not without resources to help us be more effective as consultants. When preparing to work or working in specific nations or cultures, we can be more effective if we become versed in their specific history, religion, current affairs, politics, institutional systems, and geography. We can also learn from other expatriates regarding what works best in a particular culture or nation and read the many resources on how its people think about relationships, time, and the environment around them. Social scientists, educators, and management researchers and practitioners have all contributed tools to help us. For example, Geert Hofstede's well-known dimensions of culture are based on research originally carried out in IBM's international branches and subsidiaries. The dimensions he has identified so far are as follows:

- Power distance—expressed as "the extent to which the less powerful members of organizations and institutions (like the family) accept and expect that power is distributed unequally";
- Individualism/collectivism—expressed as the degree to which the ties between individuals mean they expect to look after only themselves and their immediate family, as opposed to collectivism, which is expressed as the degree to which people from birth onwards are integrated into strong, cohesive in-groups, often extended families, which continue protecting them in exchange for loyalty;
- Masculinity/femininity—expressed in how social roles are distributed between the genders;
- Uncertainty avoidance—expressed as the extent to which a society tolerates ambiguity or uncertainty.[9]

More recently, Hofstede has added long-term versus short-term orientation and indulgence versus restraint orientation based on research by Chinese scholars.[10] This orientation is expressed in how societies look at the search for virtue and truth. Societies oriented toward the short term are less inclined than those oriented toward the long term to save for the future or persevere to get results. The U.S., for example, ranks below average and China ranks very high on long-term orientation. Societies oriented toward indulgence permit comparatively unrestrained gratification of basic human drives, whereas those oriented toward restraint suppress such gratification and have strict social norms.

In a similar effort, the Global Leadership and Organizational Behavior Effectiveness study (GLOBE) attempted to identify dimensions of leadership, which the researchers believe are culturally specific. They established nine cultural dimensions:

1. Assertiveness: "tough, confrontational, assertive and competitive versus modest and tender"; "value the strong and the winner" versus preferring "warm and cooperative relations and harmony."
2. Future orientation: "future-oriented behaviors such as planning, investing in the future, and delaying gratification" versus "instant gratification."
3. Gender differentiation: "maximizes gender role differences," according men a higher social status than women.
4. Uncertainty avoidance: "reliance on social norms and procedures to alleviate the unpredictability of future events. . . . [M]embers seek orderliness, consistence, structure, formalized procedures and laws to cover situations in their daily lives."
5. Power distance: "degree to which members of a society expect power to be unequally shared. . . . [E]xtent to which a community maintains inequality among its members by stratification of individuals and groups with respect to power, authority, prestige, status, wealth, and material possessions."
6. Collectivism versus individualism in institutions: "degree to which individuals are encouraged by societal institutions to be integrated into groups within organizations and the society. . . ." Collectivism emphasizes "allocating resources and making opportunities available for members of the society to participate in societal legislative, economic, social, and political processes."
7. In-group collectivism: "the extent to which members of a society take pride in membership in small groups such as their family and circle of close friends, and the organizations in which they are employed."
8. Performance orientation: "the degree to which a society encourages and rewards group members for performance improvement and excellence" versus emphasizes "loyalty and belonging" and "view[s] feedback as discomforting, emphasize[s] tradition, and pay[s] attention to one's family and background rather than performance."
9. Humane orientation: "encourages and rewards individuals for being fair, altruistic, generous, caring, and kind to others."[11]

In the Japanese incident described earlier, we can see both the dimensions of individualism versus collectivism and performance orientation in play. And such dimensions are not just "skin deep." In a study by Zhu and colleagues, for example, Chinese participants showed more neural activation in their brains when reflecting on themselves and their mothers, whereas Western participants only showed heighted activation when thinking about themselves.[12]

In the similar vein, management consultants Fons Trompenaars and Charles Hampden-Turner identified seven dimensions of culture based on their research with 46,000 managers in 40 nations. They concluded that people from different cultures are distinguished by where they fall along these dimensions. The dimensions are (1) universalism versus particularism; (2) individualism versus communitarianism; (3) specific versus diffuse; (4) neutral versus emotional; (5) achievement versus ascription; (6) sequential time versus synchronous time; and (7) internal direction versus outer direction.[13]

While these dimensions can be used as a heuristic for reflecting on the possible cultural influences on our own and others' values, beliefs, and behaviors, they oversimplify the diversity of national practices and organizations.[14] Even within cultures, local variations exist, and individual socializations may include organization, occupation, family, religion, tribe, gender, social class, and generation among others. Additionally, the increasing number of people with transcultural backgrounds means that people and societies are increasingly "mashups"[15] of multiple cultural and social influences. Finally, these dimensions were the results of research by North Americans and Western Europeans. We do not know if researchers from other parts of the world would identify similar dimensions.

Negotiating Cultures

This increasing cultural complexity and the difficulty in recognizing how our own thinking and behaviors are socially conditioned create a fertile ground for cultural and interpersonal misunderstandings. The risks increase of stumbling into misunderstandings and having our plans fail miserably. For consultants, cultural complexity can make us wonder how we can possibly get the outcomes our clients aspire to achieve in the world of mirrors we enter in international/intercultural settings. What strategies can we use to be more skillful at negotiating cultures and situations in which we aren't sure what "the rules of the game" are?

To illustrate both these challenges and how they might be negotiated, Brooks writes of her personal experience of consulting in Southeast Asia and then analyzes the experience drawing on Hofstede's work. What is evident in her description is how the assumptions we bring with us from our own culture may set us up for failure if we have not developed skills to help us work in situations where "our way" is not "the way."

> I grew up in the U.S. in an American family of northern European decent. I tend to value equality and respect professional competence. I also don't naturally give deference to hierarchy. It's just not how I was raised. I expect administrators to support the professionals in their organizations to do the best job they can and not interfere.
>
> Recently, I did a workshop for a Southeast Asian university to help faculty develop research proposals for an upcoming infusion of money from the World Bank. Or at least that was how the workshop was described to me when I agreed to do it. However, when I arrived, the 12 faculty members I had been told would attend the workshop had mushroomed to 25 and included staff members who were not going to be doing research. Within the first few minutes, the university president, who was also at the workshop, had outlined what he saw to be the purpose of the workshop (nothing to do with research) and established what the workshop process would be. He then looked at me expectantly and waited for me to do it.
>
> I was caught between the president, the university faculty, the expatriate who had originally asked me to do the workshop, and what I knew the World Bank was going to expect these faculty members to produce in order to get their research funded.
>
> Experiencing at least as much stress as I was, was the faculty leader (also acting as the interpreter), a member of the information technology faculty. He was not only interpreting back and forth between English and his own language, but was trying to mediate between my understanding of the workshop and the cultural expectation that we comply with the university president's wishes. He was caught in the middle, trying to negotiate all expectations.

This story illustrates that the adage "expect the unexpected" is especially apt when we are out of our own familiar cultural milieu. However, it does not communicate the "out of control" feeling and confusion that often are part of such work. Brooks provides more detail about what took place:

> The faculty leader whom I had been communicating with as I developed the workshop warned me when I arrived for the workshop that the number of attendees had doubled. I immediately started strategizing in my mind how I would need to adapt the workshop. I figured that I would go to the classroom where the workshop was being held about 30 minutes early to set up the room and make sure the technology was working. But instead of doing that, representatives of the university wanted to take us on a tour of the university, which meant we didn't actually get to the classroom until about five minutes before the workshop was to start. And then, the computer connection didn't work.
>
> After a 30-minute delay, during which the staff tried to get the technology working, I began the workshop by welcoming everyone, especially the president of the university. The president then told me (and everybody else) what he expected the workshop to address. It was not at all what I had been

contracted to do or what I had worked out with the faculty leader. The faculty leader himself looked really nervous. In an aside, I told him that I had not made preparations to do what the president wanted and didn't have the information with me that the group would need. As I contemplated the looming three-hour gulf of time during which the entire group expected me to do something meaningful for them and the unexpected change in the purpose of the workshop, my throat tightened, and I could feel myself perspiring in the tropical heat.

At that point, I had the lucky presence of mind to just "give up." I turned to the faculty leader (who was standing next to me as interpreter) and asked him what he thought we should do. We agreed to let the large group divide itself into smaller groups to work, and we would coach the groups. As I watched the interpreter coach one of the groups, I realized that the interpreter himself had most if not all of the skills and experience that were needed to run the workshop. In another aside to the interpreter, I said this to him. He acknowledged that it was true, but that as a young faculty member, he did not have the "face" to conduct this workshop and needed someone like me, older and from a respected U.S. university, to do it.

From that point on, we began to work as a team. I focused on not only coaching small groups, but also on transferring credibility to the faculty leader. I shifted my internal goal to helping to transition power from me, an expatriate, to the university's own faculty.

Near the close of the workshop, a few of the groups shared what they had worked on, carefully negotiating their presentations between the expectations of the president, the faculty leader, and me. And in working with individual groups, I managed to highlight the importance of justifying funding requests with data, preparing a realistic budget, and addressing funder expectations of financial accountability.

This story is complicated by the power imbalances between the "global north"—or richer, more industrialized nations—and the "global south," or nations that were previously colonized or are characterized by economic poverty. It is also made more complex by the tension between the agendas of donors from the global north and borrowers and aid recipients from the global south. Organizations like the World Bank have been criticized for hiring consultants from nations in the global north in preference to and for higher pay than well-qualified local consultants, who when hired, are paid less.[16]

Antal and Friedman describe the awareness and set of competencies we can use when working in culturally unfamiliar settings. These include

> an active awareness of oneself as a complex cultural being and the effect of one's own culture on thinking and action, an ability to engage with others to explore tacit assumptions that underlie behavior and goals, and an openness to testing out different ways of thinking and doing things. These competencies enable people to discover differing views of reality, making it more likely that they will create common understandings and generate collaborative action.[17]

They tag these competencies as "negotiating reality." When negotiating reality, "individuals must have an active awareness of how their own cultural backgrounds influence their perceptions and behavior, an ability to engage with others to explore assumptions, and an openness to trying out different ways of seeing and doing things." The concept is grounded in three beliefs: "(1) all people are of equal importance and worthy of equal respect; (2) as cultural beings, people differ because they possess different repertoires of ways of seeing and doing things; and (3) the repertoire of no individual or group merits a priori superiority or right to dominance."[18]

They offer three questions for analyzing what is taking place in complex and often confounding cultural interactions: (a) How do I (they) perceive the situation? (b) What do I (they) wish to achieve in this situation? (c) Which strategy do I (they) intend to employ to achieve my goals?

Here Brooks analyzes her experience with the university in Southeast Asia using these questions:

(a) *How do I (they) perceive the situation?*

Consultant: I will not be able to do what I had planned.

Interpreter: We will not be able to do what had been planned, and I am going to have to work between the president's and the foreigner's expectations.

President: I will tell them what we need to do to develop the university; I must assure my faculty that I am knowledgeable and in charge and think about what the national ministry is expecting, too.

(b) *What do I (they) wish to achieve in this situation?*

Consultant: I want to help faculty members develop their capacity to do research.

Interpreter: I want to keep both the rector and the foreigner happy.

President: I want the faculty to see that I have a plan, and I want them to move forward with my plan.

(c) *Which strategy do I (they) intend to employ to achieve my goals?*

Consultant: I will work with the interpreter and faculty to adapt the workshop and try and figure out how we can all be successful. I will adapt the workshop to communicate respect for the president and help those faculty members who are capable and interested to develop research proposals.

Interpreter: I will work with the foreigner to adapt the workshop and help her to understand what is going on. I will manage the situation to maintain respect for the president.

President: I will outline what we are to do, explain why we are doing it, give specific directions, provide context for the workshop, and tell them what my expectations are of them.

Skills for Negotiating Cultures

Consultants draw their credibility and skill at working outside of their own cultures from different sources. Some consultants have grown up in two or more cultures and speak more than one language. They may act as *boundary spanners* as they use their culture and language knowledge to translate between groups. Others have accrued extended experience in a specific culture, nation, or region of the world, becoming "specialists" in particular contexts. They draw their credibility and skill from their depth of knowledge and experience, and the web of people within a particular culture or nation with whom they have worked. Others "drop into" different cultures or nations, doing more or less the same work in each one. Still others develop extensive networks of local consultants from various nations or cultural groups and partner with them on projects.

No matter how much general experience we've gained working together with people with whom we share few cultural affinities, most of us are still challenged when we encounter situations we didn't expect and don't understand, and at the same time in which we feel responsible for ensuring a positive outcome. We all can lose our bearings when we work in unfamiliar cultural settings among people whose language we don't understand or whose language we somewhat understand, but speak imperfectly. These moments are more common than not. Particular personal abilities and skills are helpful in negotiating our own reactions and the culture we are encountering in these stressful moments.

Box 6.1 Skills for working in transcultural settings

- Tolerating ambiguity, uncertainty, and not knowing
- Gathering and analyzing information
- Suspending judgment and staying open to further learning
- Tolerating lack of control
- Cultivating patience to watch situations evolve
- Recognizing that others probably see the world differently than we do
- Seeing that others probably hold stereotypes about one or more of our identities, such as our gender, age, ethnicity/race, or country of origin
- Reflecting on our own thinking and feelings
- Expecting the unexpected

Box 6.2. What to investigate when we enter an unfamiliar cultural setting

- How to dress
- How to deal with people
- Punctuality
- When and how to start discussions
- Written and/or oral communication
- Formal and informal interpretation
- The use of go-betweens
- Display or restraint of emotion
- What language and terms to use (and not to use)
- Taboos
- How to address people

Focusing specifically on what we can *do* to prepare, Milan Kubr offers a list of behaviors we might investigate regarding an unfamiliar setting.

The list of "skills" that we've identified based on looking at the success of international consultants seems to include strong reflection, self-monitoring processes, and information-gathering. These skills are very similar to the "self" processes identified by psychologist Michael Heatherton in a review of neuroscience research on what people do in order to avoid being ousted from a group.[19] He identifies four components that allow people to modify what they do in the service of avoiding expulsion from the group, the last thing a consultant wants to have happen. They are *self-awareness*, *theory of mind*, *threat detection*, and *self-regulation*. Self-awareness is the ability to reflect on one's behaviors, including emotional displays, in order to judge them against the norms of a particular group. Theory of mind refers to the ability to make inferences about others' mental states so as to predict their actions. Threat detection speaks to our ability to monitor our environment for signs of potential group exclusion. Self-regulation refers to our ability, once we become aware that others are negatively evaluating us, to change the situation so as to rebuild good relations with others in the group. He writes,

> Doing so requires . . . people to change according to social context, including altering their thoughts, actions, and emotions. Thus, people need to inhibit their impulses, stifle their desires, resist temptations, undertake difficult or unpleasant activities, banish unwanted and intrusive thoughts, and control their emotional displays, all of which are difficult to do but are necessary to stay in the good graces of others.[20]

While this research does not tell us whether or not we can develop our abilities to use these four components, it does provide evidence of differences between those socialized in collectivist versus individualist cultures.

Consulting in Diverse Groups

While the upswing in international consulting draws our attention to the differences and similarities between national cultures and the particular knowledge and personal skills that can enhance our chances of success, we are also more likely to work with client groups comprised of people who come from a potpourri of different cultural backgrounds and bring diverse identities. One manager of Mexican heritage working on a credit and underwriting project told this story of working with others from the United States who were socialized into the dominant culture of U.S. business:

> In Mexican culture, you're always supposed to be humble. So whether you understand something or not, you're supposed to put it in the form of a question. You have to keep it open-ended, out of respect. I think that actually worked against me, because the Americans thought I really didn't know what I was talking about. So it made me feel like they thought I was wavering on my answer.[21]

Those who identify with mainstream U.S. work culture are more likely to demonstrate and assert their knowledge, both to work more efficiently and to demonstrate their competence and justify their position. They are also likely to misinterpret the behaviors of those who do not share their socialization.

Such diversity is not just based in the cultural group in which we were raised. Each of us has also been socialized to a "collective mental programming" particular to groups characterized by such qualities as gender, age cohort, occupational group, economic social class, race, and ethnicity. Significant literature exists on diversity in organizations, as well as numerous consultants and consultancy firms that specialize in diversity. For those of us who do not specialize in consulting about diversity in organizations, we must still be able to work among diverse members of organizations. While such diversity has been found to potentially contribute to a group's creativity, potential for conflict may also grow. As consultants, our tendency is to not listen well to those who have a different "mental programming" than we do. This means we not only need to remain alert to our own patterns of listening and "tuning out"—we may also need to help our clients become better listeners when working with those who do not see the world in the same way as they do.

Power inequalities within our client organizations or communities may also contribute to relationships among members and groups that are infused with resentment, arrogance, defensiveness, and blindness in relation to others in the group. For example, in many organizations, those in finance may hold more group power than those in marketing. In teams, engineers and managers may dominate those with less education. Men may assume more right to speak than women. Similarly, in communities, individuals from the business sector may assume the privilege to be listened to over those from the nonprofit sector. The list could go on, but for consultants, if we are concerned with both maximizing the knowledge we bring to the project and our success in implementing whatever plan we come up with, these power differences are important.

Transcultural/Transnational Identities

People who identify with more than one nation, culture, language, or other group to which they have socialized constitute an increasing segment of the world's population. Immigration and life experiences such as studying, working, or being raised in another region as an expatriate are also sources of socialization. This complicates *this* culture versus *that* culture understandings.

In a personal example, Brooks's daughter, who was born in Japan to an American mother and a New Zealand father and recently married a man from Switzerland whom she met on vacation in Panama while working in Costa Rica for a Fair Trade coffee plantation, is no longer an anomaly. What's more, bicultural or transcultural individuals like this, according to studies, seem to switch between cultural frames,[22] making it difficult to either know or predict how they will think or behave in new situations. Whether or not we consider ourselves transcultural or multilingual, most of us draw on the several cultural configurations to which we have been socialized and so have a repertoire of ways of thinking and acting, which we use, mostly unconsciously, according to the community in which we need to be culturally competent. Thus, all of us carry with us, usually at a subconscious level, sets of beliefs and assumptions that we take for granted, rarely examining them. These beliefs and assumptions profoundly influence how we perceive the world and how we act in our day-to-day lives.

Transcultural/transnational individuals can draw on and refer to multiple cultural, linguistic, and experiential resources in their work and lives. If as consultants we are lucky enough to have had such rich life experiences, we can act as boundary spanners between specific cultures and languages, and we can more effectively work in multiple cultural and national settings. Surprisingly, organizations and communities often overlook such persons as the valuable resource they are.

Brooks recalls being called in by a major U.S. technology company in the late 1990s to consult on its work in Japan:

> I remember being shocked by the presence of two Japanese Americans on the client team, one of whom spoke fluent Japanese. How, I wondered, could the company be overlooking these valuable resources? I was also astonished that the company relied on a Japanese national provided by their Japanese company counterpart for all interpreting and translation between the two languages. Why didn't the company provide their own interpreters? Did they imagine that interpreting in such negotiations was neutral? I mentioned this to the Japanese American who was fluent in Japanese, and he just shrugged.

Fortunately, organizations, nations, and consultants are becoming more cognizant of the disadvantages they accrue by remaining culturally and linguistically uneducated.

Conclusion

Edgar Schein was right in 1969 when he gave us the idea and the practice of process consultation. While initially taken up by those in the field of organizational development, the concern with the human dimension of organizations is increasingly relevant for all consultants. Technical expertise is important, but unless it is brought together with expertise in human processes, it is increasingly likely to be regarded with skepticism or discounted altogether as irrelevant to the particular organization or community. This is particularly true in the international context where information and expertise are ever more available via the Internet and local experts, who bring a wealth of expertise from the most prestigious educational and business institutions in the world. As Jawaharlal Nehru pointed out in his reflections on visiting America,

> It is not easy for a person of one country to enter into the background of another country. So there is great irritation because one fact that seems obvious to us is not immediately accepted by the other party or does not seem obvious to him at all. . . . In order to understand them, we have to understand their way of life and approach. If we wish to convince them, we have to use their language as far as we can, not language in the narrow sense of the word, but the language of the mind. That is the one necessity. Something that goes even further than that is not the appeal to logic and reason, but some kind of emotional awareness of other people.[23]

In the next section, we discuss specific inquiry skills consultants can use when working in organizations, communities, and nations to make their work more contextually relevant, responsive, and appropriate, and thus more likely to achieve intended outcomes.

Part III

Skills of Inquiry

Inquiry has two main goals in a consulting project—learning the organization and achieving the outcome. The first goal of inquiry, to learn about our client, is intentional but informal. Through this inquiry, consultants ground our own knowledge in the realities of a specific, unique organization or community. The second focus of a consulting inquiry is collecting data and information and transforming them into the knowledge needed to achieve our clients' intended outcomes. This inquiry needs to be formal and systematic. At the basis of each of these types of inquiry are the skills of listening and asking questions. Part III focuses on the specific skills required to carry out inquiry as consultants.

Chapter 7, "Facilitating Inquiry," looks closely at the skills of listening and asking questions. We examine the purposes of these two skills and the higher-order skill of deciding when and how to use them. While we place this chapter together with our chapters on how to carry out inquiry, these skills are equally as valuable at every other juncture of the consulting process.

Chapter 8, "Learning the Organization," recognizes that while knowledge can be adapted to specific contexts, each context is unique. Thus, consultants' work, if we are actually to take on the challenge of working together with our clients to achieve outcomes, requires us to know exactly who our clients are as individuals, as groups, and as organizations or communities, and in ever-shifting economic, social, and political contexts. Otherwise, as we point out in this chapter, we may find ourselves "playing checkers when everyone in the organization or community is playing chess." The board looks the same, but the rules are vastly different.

Finally, Chapter 9, "Methods of Inquiry," discusses the tools of formal inquiry. While "Learning the Organization" focuses on the informal inquiry we carry out as consultants to understand our clients and their world, "Methods of Inquiry" considers the tools we need to gather the data and information, analyze, and interpret what we have gathered. This is the evidence that serves as a basis for the action steps, tactics, and strategies we use to achieve outcomes. Again, this is formal and systematic work. Without careful application of inquiry skills, our conclusions may be flawed. Scientists and researchers have honed these methods and skills over decades to yield trustworthy and valid results. This is the evidence on which we need to base our conclusions and actions.

7

Facilitating Inquiry

It is not enough to rely on our expert knowledge. Expert knowledge is necessary but not sufficient. We have to learn how to ask ourselves totally different questions.

—Reg Revans, *The ABC of Action Learning*

Asking questions and listening are at the heart of learning and inquiry. From the time we are small children, as humans we ask questions in order to learn. If we think we already know and don't need to ask questions or listen, then we are cutting off learning and inquiry into how things are and, as importantly, how things can be better.

Asking questions and listening are also at the heart of consulting and, as many have stated, essential to good leadership. They are skills that often don't come naturally to professionals who have been socialized to "know" and to "tell" others what we know. In fact, we might wonder, "Why would anyone in a profession that gets paid to have expert knowledge ever *want* to ask a question and listen instead of giving an answer?" If we are accustomed to giving advice and selling our ideas and products, we rarely see a need to ask a question or listen.

For consultants, knowing the answer is usually why we were hired. The precondition for our work is our knowledge and expertise, and we are prepared to share it. However, one of the most disturbing experiences for clients is for a consultant to not listen to or understand them. In the words of one client, a university vice president, as she reflected on a recent experience with consultants, "It's a real sinking feeling to share a problem and tell them what we want and to see they are not really listening. They were very attentive, but just to see what I'm saying so they can use that to convince me to do what they want to do."[1]

Several reasons exist as to why asking questions is so central to the practice of consulting. Questions help build our relationship with our clients, increase the information we have available to inform our work

Table 7.1 The usefulness of listening and asking questions

Build Client-Consultant Relationships	*Increase Information*	*Strengthen Divergent Thinking*	*Strengthen Convergent Thinking*	*Increase Capacity*
• Increase consultant credibility • Build trust • Strengthen trust	• Make tacit knowledge explicit • Elicit information • Clarify clients' thinking	• Enable analysis • Verify conclusions • Focus thinking	• Hone analysis • Verify conclusions • Focus thinking	• Embed process to outcome in organization/community • Transfer inquiry skills

towards achieving the outcome, strengthening the quality of client/consultant thinking processes, and increasing client capacity (Table 7.1).

In the following sections, we will look at the skills that go into both listening and asking questions.

The Courage to Listen

Listening, of course, takes courage. It requires us to be open to the possibility that our clients may throw a wrench into our works. They may introduce something that we aren't prepared for or that doesn't fit our plans or sense of our own competence. Consulting projects can easily founder on the consultant's lack of knowledge—not a lack of expert knowledge, but a lack of knowledge about particular clients. In the words of one client we interviewed, a university vice president, "As the client, I know what the presenting problem is. Of course I recognize that there is always a presenting problem, but it is not always *the* problem. How it gets framed and identified and described by the consultant is crucial. How responsive the consultant can be to my situation. I may not know exactly what the problem is, but you have to let me identify it. You have to listen to me."

Listening to our clients and asking them good questions are not only at the heart of working together with our clients, they are key to sparking learning, innovation, and knowledge creation. They are not skills that come naturally to most of us, but they are ones we can develop.

The Benefits of Listening

Listening is the foundation of learning about our clients and their worlds. As our clients talk with us, we learn what they value and what threatens them, whom they view as influential or troubling, what they think is possible and the barriers they perceive, and what language and words have special meaning to the organization or community.

Listening to our clients is also the most effective and powerful way of developing relationships with them. As we listen to their joys and worries, we are communicating not just that we are interested in them, but that we care about them. As they tell us their stories and find us to be concerned listeners, they begin to gain trust in us. Listening to our clients tells them that we are going to work *with* them to achieve the outcomes *they* want, rather than treat them as just one more client. Researching adult development, Belenky, Clinchy, Goldberger, and Tarule write, "Really listening and suspending one's own judgment is necessary in order to understand other people on their own terms. . . . This is a process that requires trust and builds trust."[2] We all share more of what we know when we believe the other person is listening.

Why We Don't Listen

For many people, consultants included, listening can be challenging. We may feel pressured by what we see as the role of consultants: to be the person with the answers. We may also be cognizant of the time pressures our clients feel, and believe that as outsiders, we need to work fast so as not to be perceived as wasting their time. We may also, quite simply, lack skill in listening, given that few universities or business schools teach it outside of counseling education. We also may have little experience in working collaboratively, have an "impatient personality," or be particularly action oriented. Our current era of video conferencing, online communication, and telephone calls doesn't necessarily foster a listening demeanor, so we may find it hard to communicate that we're listening. We may also experience strong emotions while working with clients, either our own or our clients', and these may hijack our focus on listening and understanding. Language limitations and differences, different cultural assumptions, and unfamiliar contexts can mean that we don't understand the deeper or even the intended meaning of what our clients are saying. In addition, we may not feel comfortable showing that we didn't quite understand the meaning of what was being said. Other barriers include thinking about what we will say while waiting for our own turn to talk, only hearing what we want to hear, and fearing that the people we are listening to are overreacting and therefore discounting what they're saying and blocking them out.

We communicate that we don't value what others say in several ways. Our eyes may glaze; we may look at others rather than the person speaking; we may look at our notes or at our cellphones; we interrupt, or fail to respond to what the other person has said. Communicating that we don't value the other varies depending on culture, and as consultants we need to be aware of our own culturally based habits and conscious that they may not be universal.

While listening may not come naturally to us, or circumstances may make listening to others a challenge, we can develop the listening skills that communicate to our clients that we respect them, and in the process increase the information and knowledge we can draw on in our efforts to achieve the outcome.

Skills for Listening

Many have delineated skills for listening. The Center for Creative Leadership,[3] for example, recently authored a book on active listening to help leaders improve their skills. They recommend that leaders pay attention, hold judgment, reflect, clarify, summarize, and share. Skills that are important for us as consultants go beyond those, since our purpose is not to lead but to co-create new knowledge and facilitate change. We identify those skills in Figure 7.1 and go on to elaborate on them.

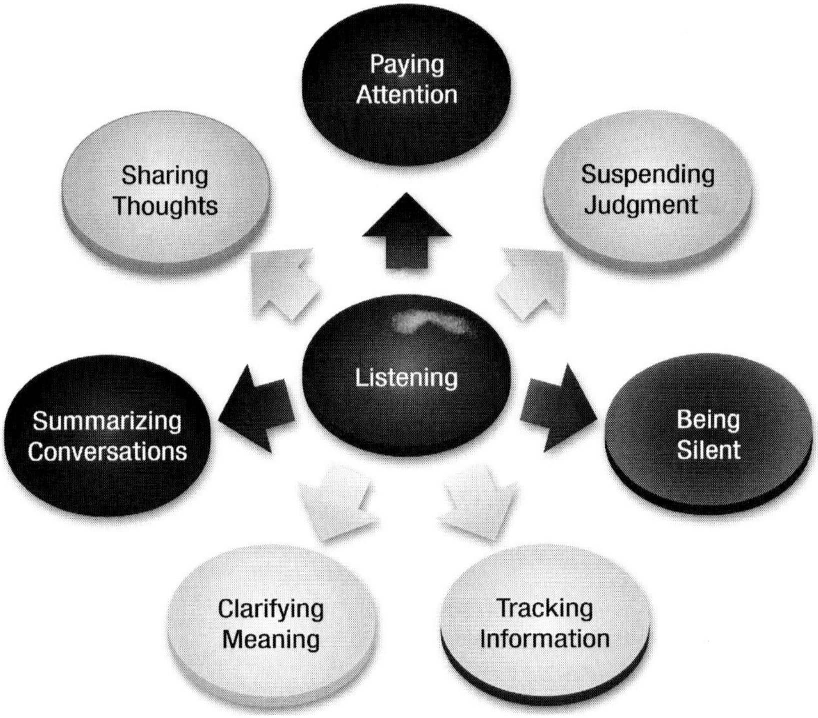

Figure 7.1 Listening skills

Paying Attention

Attention can be defined as the application of the mind to any object of sense or thought. It implies a focusing of consciousness to produce greater vividness and clarity.[4] Mindfulness, which we address in Chapter 3, is defined as paying attention in the present moment.[5] When we pay attention, we allow ourselves to be silent and get ready to summarize what the other person's ideas, concerns, and feelings are.

Suspending Judgment

Suspending judgment is key to developing an open and inquiring mindset. Suspending judgment does not mean that we agree with what someone is saying, rather that we are trying to understand instead of judge. What we have to offer is acceptance of the other person and respect for his or her perspective. Patience and silence are at the heart of this skill.

Reflecting

Reflecting refers to paraphrasing information or checking out a feeling with someone. When we reflect, we are making sure we are tracking what the person has said or is feeling. It has the effect of assuring the person who's speaking that we understand him or her and his or her perspective, as well as encouraging the person to provide additional information or detail ("It sounds like you're not sure we should implement this," or "So you're saying that you don't think marketing are behind this?").

Clarifying

Clarifying has much the same purpose as reflecting. When we clarify, we ask open-ended questions to help understand better or paraphrase what we thought we heard and check to see if we understood it accurately.

Summarizing

Summarizing is useful at significant shifting points. By identifying the main themes of what has been said and stating what we understand each person's actions will be, we can make sure everyone present is on the same page and establish a group understanding and commitment. Summarizing can also encourage speakers to clarify or elaborate so that we better understand.

Silence

While each of these techniques help to elicit our clients' thoughts, silence is often the most powerful technique in facilitating inquiry. Silence creates the space for each of us to hear our own thoughts and formulate our ideas. Out of silence can come creativity, deeper reflection, and the new knowledge that may take us to the outcome.

Sharing

Finally, once we are sure we have elicited and understood others' information and views, we can share our own: "While I was listening to you, I was reminded of. . . ." We also share in the context of serving as an information and knowledge resource for our clients.

The Power of Questions: What Are the Benefits of Asking Questions?

If listening is hard for many of us, asking questions can be even harder. Much of education is organized to convey information and knowledge and then check that we've learned it, producing a cadre of people who believe they've performed badly if they don't know the answer. As adults, at work or as parents, we often feel that others expect us to know the answers. Asking questions or not being able to answer a question seems to say that we are not competent in our role. We may also avoid asking questions because we want to maintain harmony in a relationship, we don't want to threaten others, or we don't want to be seen as wasting everyone's time. As consultants, we may be very uncomfortable with the uncertainty that asking questions invites. So we build our products, services, and advice based on our professional knowledge and what has worked for us in the past.

Questions help us to confront the world "as it is," what Jim Collins calls in *From Good to Great* "the brutal facts."[6] By not asking questions, we maintain our illusion that reality is as we think it is and screen out information we don't want to hear. Marquardt uses the sinking of the Titanic, the Bay of Pigs invasion in the Kennedy era, and the explosion of the *Challenger* spacecraft as examples of disasters that could have been prevented. If the experts in all of those situations had asked more questions and questioned more assumptions, many lives might have been saved.

Questions help lift both clients and consultants out of "the way things are" and open the door to "the way things can be." We can gain distance on the habitual ways things are done, the routines, and the unquestioned assumptions. They help us to spot opportunities and threats. Our clients' answers tell us what they know and think about the challenges they're facing. They also paint a picture for us of the people, the organization or the community, the values and beliefs, the political landscape, and the difficulties our clients have already faced and that have raised the particular issue we are hoping to address with them to a level that is important enough that they have contacted us. Our clients' responses spark the conversations that lead to the creation of new knowledge.

How Do We Make the Leap from Having Answers to Having Questions?

Shifting from telling or giving advice to asking questions requires a leap in thinking. In fact, for consultants and other knowledge workers who are "supposed to know," it may seem counter-intuitive: "If I think I already know what they should do, why don't I tell them?" But if we are concerned with achieving outcomes, bringing as much relevant knowledge, resources, and support as we can to a project, and then making new knowledge and learning a part of the organization or community, we need to engage our clients in inquiry. The most efficient way of doing that is to ask questions that engage our clients in the process and elicit relevant information.

Asking good questions requires that we constantly analyze with a mind open to integrating new information, as together with our clients we try to figure out the best way to get where we're going. What do we know? What do we need to find out? Shifting from knowing and telling to inquiring, bringing in new information, and integrating it into new knowledge asks that we shift the way we think about and interact with our clients and what they know.

Recalling the client quoted at the beginning of this chapter and how she viewed her consultant, we can imagine two prototypical mindsets with which consultants might approach their clients: open and closed. Speaking to leaders about the value of questions, Marquardt identified these same mindsets.[7] We have adapted his typology for consultants (Table 7.2).

Table 7.2 Mindsets about the consultant-client relationship

Transactional/judging	*Partnering/inquiring*
Clients as objects of change	Clients as partners in achieving outcome
Debates	Dialogues
Listens for: Right/wrong Agree/disagree	Listens for: Information Understanding
Feedback seen as rejection	Feedback seen as more information
Gives answers and defends them	Asks questions and contributes information
Sees clients as resisting	Sees clients as knowing something we don't know

In fact, most of us exhibit both open and closed mindsets at different times, depending on the persons with whom we are interacting, how we are feeling on any given day, and of course, our beliefs and assumptions about the consultant role. However, a partnering relationship aimed at creating the knowledge needed to achieve a specific outcome mostly requires a mindset that is open. And since a closed mindset, ironically enough, has been cultivated in many graduate-level professional programs, particularly in business, medicine, engineering, and law, for example, approaching our clients with an open mind requires self-awareness, mindfulness, and skill development. We address these in Chapter 3 in our discussion of mindfulness.

Rebalancing from a predominantly closed to a more open mindset regarding knowledge is not automatic. In fact, changing our practice, little by little, is often more effective at changing habits than trying to change our mindset is. Practicing asking questions is one technique that can transform our mindset both toward knowledge and toward our clients. Asking clients good questions can be transformative for both clients and consultants because the insights that result can lead to new outcomes. Questions are the door to innovation. As Albert Einstein, one of the world's great innovators, said, "The important thing is not to stop questioning."[8]

Questions That Help Inquiry

Asking good questions is a learned skill for many consultants, and it is also a skill that consultants can help their clients learn. Practitioners of action learning have contributed much to developing the art of asking questions as a means of solving problems. Action learning is a specialized form of inquiry, originally developed by Reg Revans,[9] in which a group of people, optimally ranging from between four and eight, work together in a cycle of questions, actions, and reflection to help each other address difficult issues in an organization. Revans was a scientist, organizational consultant, Cambridge University professor, and Olympic athlete. His own transformation into a questioner began while he was at Cavendish Laboratory at Cambridge University. More than a dozen of those with whom he worked went on to become Nobel laureates. What struck him about their meetings was that the participants brought a spirit "of struggle with the unknown, the bartering of ignorance, the quest to uncover another layer of particle physics only to find themselves presented with even more ignorance."[10] What struck Revans was the participants' struggle, spirit, personal change through the process, humility, and acknowledgement of their own ignorance. They saw the boundaries of their own knowledge, and they understood that until they acknowledged and accepted these, they could make no further knowledge. Yuri Boshyk and Robert Dilworth note that this attitude is "quite contrary to the modern ethos of academic certitude and management consultant infallibility."[11]

The kinds of questions that facilitate inquiry are genuine requests for information. Important information for consultants to acquire has to do with the resources and barriers that are relevant to getting to the outcome, the history regarding the particular outcome in the organization or community, the current situation regarding the outcome, how our clients view the outcome and current situation and how they think others in the organization view the outcome and situation, and what assumptions exist that are foreclosing the chances of reaching the outcome.

O'Neil and Marsick suggest several types of questions and give examples.[12] We've drawn on and adapted their work and added additional examples in Box 7.1. The list can provide a "cheat sheet" to help us thoroughly explore a situation with our clients.

Box 7.1 Types and examples of questions

Informational Questions

What's been tried so far?
What's been the result?
Who are the key people involved?
Who else has information on that?
Who else could help with this?
What happened?

Reflective Questions

What do you think isn't working?
What do you think is getting in the way?
What do you think would happen if we were to ask why the organization continues to do X?
Why do you think this strategy has been effective?
What were the highs? What were the lows?
What *could* you do?
What difference do you think it would make if it were a different person/time/place?

Affective

How would we feel if our recommendation caused people to lose their jobs?

Probing

What is happening here?
Can you talk about that a little more?
What's an example of that?

Interpretive

What do you think the result would be?
What do you think is really going on?
How do you think others in the organization/community would respond to this?
Who do you think might/might not support this?

Challenging

Why does it have to be that way?
Why can't that be done?
What's stopping us from X?

Connecting

What would be the impact on the bottom line if we were to do X?
How would X affect customers?
How would X group have to change if we did Y?
What would be the impact on the environment/community?

Decisional

What shall we do next?
What actions are we going to take before our next meeting?
What resources do we need?
Who's going to talk to her/him/them?
How can we make the problem different?

Questions That Shut Down Inquiry

Not all questions help further the inquiry, of course. In fact, some can actually hurt the inquiry process and shut down learning. "Why" questions, for example, can imply that someone needs to justify his or her action. They can also imply blame, suggesting the person made a mistake others wouldn't have made. A less threatening way to get at the same information might be to ask what happened or how it happened. Questions that force people to defend themselves or react can easily shift the focus from trying to achieve an outcome to establishing who is right or wrong, breaking down the ethos of partnership and sliding into an ethos of competition.

Another way we might misuse questions is to *bombard* clients with them, particularly once we get on a "knowledge and information seeking" roll. As the term suggests, the persons being questioned can often feel as though they are the targets of a barrage of gunfire. Similarly, drawing again on a gun metaphor, *double-barreled* questions fold multiple requests for information into a single question—for example, "Can you describe how this happened, who was involved, and what the result was?" The person expected to answer often has trouble knowing where to begin addressing the question and then, feeling overwhelmed, answers only part of it.

Leading questions like, "Have you tried X?" or "What would happen if you did X?" are often advice disguised as inquiry. When we ask leading questions we are usually trying to force our own agenda or attempting to push agreement. Open-ended questions like, "What have you tried?" or "What else could you try?" keep the inquiry framed in our clients' contexts rather than our own.

Asking open-ended questions is the key to enabling creative inquiry. Who, what, when, where, and how all allow those trying to answer the question to bring whatever knowledge or information they think is relevant and to structure what they know (or don't know) in whatever way makes sense to them. This is a valuable resource for consultants as we work together with our clients to make the changes in the organization or community that will be needed to achieve the outcome.

Structuring Inquiry to Bring in Untapped Knowledge

If we recognize that knowledge does not just belong to the consultant or to the people "in charge" and that the individuals closest to the "action" probably have a more accurate, informed, and fine-tuned understanding of the local situation, then listening regardless of the value we assign particular persons becomes more crucial to the co-production of knowledge.[13] Not recognizing that knowledge is distributed among people throughout organizations or communities means we may be missing some of the most important information for accomplishing our goals. As consultants we need as much information about our clients and specific stakeholder groups as possible. Our clients themselves are often uninformed about what different stakeholders in their organizations or communities know or think. The information we gather is essential to developing workable tactics, strategies, and action plans to get to outcomes.

For example, in one case, school principals overlooked the "insider knowledge" that paraprofessionals in a public school could contribute to the goal of student success. As members of a low-power group, what they knew was easy for those above them in a hierarchy to overlook. The researcher on this case commented, "[The paraprofessionals'] first-hand knowledge of the school community was a unique perspective. Most of them had children attending either the schools they worked in or nearby schools. The surprising part was, they were minimally involved or rarely asked to provide input on how students within these schools might learn best."[14] Thus, the will to listen is rooted in the humility of acknowledging that while we may know our own worlds exceptionally well, we are limited in our knowledge of the worlds of others and are dependent upon what they know for our projects, programs, and policies.

Gathering information from across organizations or communities requires that the persons providing the information feel safe. Feeling unsafe can grow out of fear of retribution, ridicule, or being discounted. Patterns regarding who speaks and who doesn't may also be firmly embedded in an organization or community and be related to attitudes regarding education, age, gender, race and ethnicity, education, and hierarchical position, for example. The following conversation epitomizes how these patterns might play out in an organization or community. This interchange took place on a team charged with reducing cycle time in a manufacturing process:

Dave:	What other ideas are there? John. Are you awake?
John (an engineer):	(with embarrassment) Yeah. I'm awake.
Dave:	Carlos. Do you have any ideas?
Carlos (a technician):	(After a long pause Carlos asks a technical question, which the chair answers.)
Dave:	Do you have any ideas, Bettina, of what we can do?
Bettina (technician):	(Responds with silence.)

Dave:	Shall we . . . ? (Makes a suggestion that is met by silence. Maria, a technician, is the only one shaking her head.)
Martha (an engineer):	(Offers some information that the chair argues down.)

In the same study, others talked about an attitude that some opinions aren't as good as others, those with more power dominating the conversation, and team members withholding negative information for fear of being associated with the problem.[15]

These behaviors are not uncommon in organizations. Amy Edmondson, in her work on organizational teams, writes: "Most people in organizations are being evaluated—whether frequently or infrequently, overtly or implicitly—in an ongoing way. The presence of others with more power or status makes the threat of evaluation especially salient, but it by no means disappears in the presence of peers and subordinates. . . ."[16] She goes on to describe why they may be hesitant to ask questions:

> First, when individuals ask questions or seek information, they run the risk of being seen as ignorant . . . .Second, when admitting (or simply calling attention to) mistakes, asking for help, or accepting the high probability of failure that comes with experimenting, people risk being seen as incompetent, whether in a narrow, particular domain, or more broadly. . . . Third, to learn and improve—as individuals and collectives—it is essential to reflect critically on current and past performance. The risk of being seen as negative often stops people from delivering critical assessments of a group or individual's performance, which limits the thoroughness and accuracy of collective reflection. . . . Fourth, to avoid disrupting or imposing upon others' time and good will, people will avoid seeking feedback, information or help.

As consultants, we can take steps to structure the inclusion of the vast, untapped individual knowledge that exists in all organizations and communities. The way we structure our inquiry helps establish a zone of safety in which participants feel safe. We have adapted Amy Edmondson's recommendations for how leaders can structure safe contexts for information and knowledge sharing to our work as consultants (Box 7.2).[17]

Box 7.2 Structuring safe knowledge-sharing environments

- Be accessible to our clients and personally involved in the work
- Model that we are "okay" with failures
- Model that we think of mistakes as an important part of the process by acknowledging our own fallibility
- Take interpersonal risks by sharing our own questions and doubts
- Take care that our language and actions do not shame our clients

- Acknowledge excellence
- Coach better performance
- Make sure lower-status persons in our client organization or community feel safe and have the opportunity to contribute what they know
- Manage power by enabling those with less power to contribute
- Manage power by limiting the dominating tendencies of high-power persons
- Make sure the outcome we are trying to reach is clear to all

The Skills of Facilitating Inquiry

Both listening and asking questions require skill and discipline. As we practice and reflect on our own work, we can improve the quality of our questions and the acuity with which we listen. But facilitating inquiry and the use of questions and listening require additional skills of us as consultants to make them effective in working with our clients towards an outcome.

Balancing Expertise and Questions

Since clients hire consultants for their expertise, to balance sharing expertise with asking questions and listening is a higher-level consultant skill. Sharing our expertise can at times enhance clients' trust that we know what we are doing. This is often helpful at the earlier stages of our relationship with our clients. However, importantly, we can also convey our expertise through the way we listen to our clients and the perceptiveness of our questions. Good questions are informed by a deep understanding of the kinds of challenges our clients are confronting.

We can also share our own information; in other words, we can serve as a resource for our clients. We can provide informal benchmarking by virtue of the breadth of organizations and communities we have seen confront similar problems. How and when we share our expertise is important. All of us have optimal learning moments, those moments when we are ready and most open to taking in and using the information and skills others have to share. Recognizing those moments and being ready to meet them moves consultants from purveyors of PowerPoint presentations, even very clever and graphic PowerPoint presentations, to skilled coaches. Skilled coaches bring out the best in their players for the good of the team. They are sensitive to giving "just-in-time" guidance and information.

Part of the skill of balancing expertise with questions lies in assessing the context. Some cultural contexts expect that their consultant will be an expert and the consultant has been hired to share that expertise. This often requires consultants to display their expertise as a platform for engaging in inquiry. In a workshop we conducted for consultants from a variety of nations and cultural backgrounds, a professional from the Middle East suggested that many in her country expected to "learn from the West." However, when questioned further about how well Western management practices fit her country, she pointed out that we need more research on the cultural practices of consulting. Lacking a body of comparative research on consulting, as consultants, we need to develop our own skill at determining the balance between simply transferring expertise and engaging in inquiry.

Knowing the Purpose

Questions can be threatening, irritating, or just a waste of time if we are not clear about our purpose in asking them. Each phase of the inquiry model of consulting has a different purpose and so requires our questions to serve a different purpose. If we are trying to help our clients formulate the outcome they want, our questions aim at helping to clarify challenges, hopes, and barriers, and finally to articulate desired outcomes. If we are engaged with a group of stakeholders during the inquiry process, the purpose of our questions may be to find out what they are doing now, what they want, what they fear, what they think would work, and what they think wouldn't work, for example. As we move toward analyzing all of the information we have and developing an action plan, our questions help to strengthen analysis, look for unintended consequences, take different perspectives, and become concrete regarding action steps. When we evaluate what we've tried, our questions are likely to focus on comparing what we have with what we hoped to achieve. As we move into sharing our knowledge beyond the group that worked on the project, our questions may aim to open up thinking and encourage creativity. And so-called "dumb" questions can be unexpectedly useful in helping clients and consultants alike to reconsider the perspective we're taking and the path we are on.

Conclusion

Questions and listening are powerful consultant skills. Indeed, they differentiate between simply passing along shopworn expertise and opening the door to a partnership that draws on both client and consultant expertise to achieve an outcome uniquely suited to each client. Questions and listening can be the difference between a consultant product or service that may be competent but is lackluster, costly, and deeply disappointing, and one that is innovative and customized. The former suits a world we imagine to be the same from one moment or one context to the next. The latter suits a world in which we are all struggling to find new ways to address the challenges rapid change and complexity are dealing us.

In the next two chapters, we draw on the skills in this chapter to focus specifically on the informal consultant inquiry of learning about the clients we serve and the more formal consultant-client co-inquiry of figuring out how to achieve the outcome.

8

Learning the Organization

If you are going to play the game properly, you'd better know every rule.

—Barbara Jordan

From the first moment we step into our client's world as consultants, we are on a learning quest. Like explorers of any new territory, we may be both exhilarated at the prospect of new discoveries and terrified by the hazards that could lie hidden along our path.

Finding Out the "Rules of the Game"

Like any sojourner in someone else's world, the more we learn about the world we've entered, the more effective our actions will be. When we don't understand the internal logic at work in our clients' worlds, we are, in a way, likely to be playing the wrong game using the wrong rules. Think playing in a chess tournament on a chessboard, but using the rules for checkers.

Not understanding the "game" can have disastrous consequences for consultants. Consider a recent assessment conducted for the United Nations[1] on why development projects to install eGovernment systems fail. The assessment report points to "the oversize gaps between project design and on-the-ground reality." Indeed, most eGovernment projects fail. For example, the report cites a scientific information system that was designed to support a natural resources ministry in East Africa in making strategic decisions. Although the system was installed and produced information, that information was for the most part ignored by decision-makers. An analysis of the project turned up four dimensions on which the project design assumptions were different from the particular reality of the ministry. On the information dimension, the system design assumed the ministry would value formal strategic information, but in reality, decision-makers used informal information and their gut feelings. On the process dimension, the system design assumed the ministry used a rational model of structured decision-making, but in reality, the ministry used personalized and even politicized unstructured decision-making. On the objectives and values dimension, the system design assumed that the ministry valued rules and logic similar to the scientific environment within which the system had been designed, whereas in reality, the ministry was a political environment characterized by a "power culture" in which self-interest and hidden agendas were valued. Finally, on the dimension of management systems and structures, the system design assumed that the ministry had both the structures and systems needed to support strategic decision-making, while in reality, they did not exist. This was a project that drew on the knowledge, experiences, and assumptions of the consultants who introduced it, but failed miserably in a context unlike that of the consultants.

Being Invited In

In order to learn the rules or the logic of our clients' worlds, we have to be invited in. This does not mean just signing a contract. As parties to a contract, we have, in a sense, just been granted a visa. Similar to when we visit another country, we may be able to use their roads and eat at their restaurants (particularly those specially designed for tourists), but our hosts will not necessarily invite us into their homes. We won't meet their families, and we are unlikely to have a chance to share in important parts of their lives if they don't believe that we respect them and intend them no harm.

Being invited in and being granted access to the inner workings of a client's organization or community is a gift. But it is a gift we are usually only offered when we are sincerely interested in the client and open to understanding how the client's world works. With curiosity and openness to learning, we begin to understand what it is like for those who live there. As we become better at speaking their language, we start to share in their jokes and struggles. They share with us the strategies they've learned to more easily navigate around their worlds, and for those of us who value food, we've moved past the restaurants in the tourist books or reviewed in international newspapers or websites and been shown the "real" places where local people eat, and been invited to share food with them in their homes. To be effective partners as consultants, this is the kind of acceptance and access we need.

"Like a Bull in a China Shop"

When we enter into an organization or community as consultants, though, we find ourselves in a paradoxical position. We are there because we bring some kind of expertise, but we usually don't know how our expertise fits or indeed how our clients will respond. We have to both maintain our own credibility and find out what we don't know, including what our clients already know about addressing challenges we may encounter along the way to achieving the goal. We bring knowledge and usually have experience with the project or task we've been hired to work on, but while we all draw on our past experience to help us with new challenges, we are faced with an organization or community that is unique and special in ways only its members know about.

Our challenge is to remain conscious of our own lenses, while at the same time being open to what we find in the organization or community. We want to start with a blank page, but the reality is that as humans, our pages are already tinted with our own preferences, strongly held beliefs, and needs to protect our own professional identity. What we find may be counterintuitive and unexpected, and contradict what we expect to find, but if we are open to the unexpected, we may discover new ways to share and apply our expertise.

At the same time, one of the biggest advantages to being an outsider in a consultant-client partnership is that we bring a fresh perspective about the organization or community. We can often notice things insiders take for granted. While outsiders like us may not understand all of the dynamics that have gone into forming a community or an organization, our naïve outsider observations can provide our clients with a different perspective on themselves and a window into "how others see us" and "how we are different" or unique. We lose this asset if we are too quick to be "the expert" and act as though our view is somehow superior to those of our clients. When we impose our own assumptions and biases on what we are seeing, we may miss the value our outsider status gives us: a different perspective and new energy that can be very helpful to those working there permanently.

Our job, then, not only when we first enter, but throughout the term of our partnership, is to be open and skilled at "learning" the organization. Our work throughout is to continue to gather and analyze information about our clients. Like sociocultural anthropologists, we observe, ask questions, reflect, and analyze. As practitioners intent on implementing effective changes, we may also tentatively experiment. In this sense, carefully listening to our clients is key. One internal consultant working in the field of diversity tells of learning the hard way to listen more than she talked:

> When I went into my first organization, I immediately started uncovering things that didn't make sense to me and needed to change. I went in like a bull in a china shop. "This is wrong. You can't do that," I said. It was a disaster. I didn't know who I was talking to. You need to know the players. You have to know the organization. I made a name for myself right away. But I'm not sure what that name was. I didn't allow for the possibility that I didn't understand. At my next job, I learned to be quieter longer.[2]

What to Look For

The best consultants have always been, like good sociocultural anthropologists, acute observers and information gatherers. Harry Levinson (2002) tells a story about working with several other consultants on a study of what was then the Kansas Power and Light Company. As they were interviewing and observing in one community, an explosion occurred:

> A gas line across the Kansas River had blown up. A gas crew was rowing toward the point of the explosion when they suddenly became aware of my colleague observer in the boat. In surprised astonishment, they wanted to know what on earth he was doing there. "Observing," he replied.[3]

Although the current consulting environment is more time constrained and the level to which Levinson immersed himself is rarely possible anymore, careful observation and ongoing information-gathering about our clients and their worlds is as crucial as ever to both the quality of our work and our credibility with clients. Edwards increased her learning of one organization when she took the time to immerse herself in the actual work employees do. She worked with a psychiatric hospital and her task was to redesign the training for new employees:

> Whenever the trainers and I would get into a discussion about what changes needed to be made, they would say, "Well, we can't do that. You've never been on the ward and so you don't know what it's like." I decided to find out and worked for a number of weekends on an acute psychiatric ward as a mental health worker. It raised my credibility with the employees. And it was a humbling experience that did indeed add to my knowledge about what training would be helpful to a new employee in that setting.

> One of my most important discoveries was that our training needed to be much more focused on application. For example, on my first day on the ward a patient collapsed right in front of me in a seizure. I had been taught the difference between a tonic and clonic seizure and other medical terminology related to seizures. But the real question in that moment was "*What do I do*?"

Where to Start?

Both organizations and communities are so complex and multifaceted that we often don't know what to find out about first when we begin our journey together. While staying conscious of the whole, for analytic purposes, looking at an organization or community through different lenses can be helpful. A common way to analyze organization is through the lenses of culture, structure, people, and power. Consultants may choose different lenses, depending on their purpose. For example, community development aimed at identifying and building on the assets in a community may learn about or analyze a community through the lenses of people, voluntary organizations, local institutions, physical assets, and economic assets.[4] Focusing here on organizations, we will first explore how we might learn enough about them to make our work relevant and avoid delivering costly but unusable services and products through the lenses mentioned above (culture, structure and processes, people, and power). We will then turn to the assets and gifts in communities and organizations that we can not only take note of, but also enlist in achieving goals and outcomes.

Cultures and Social Groups in Organizations and Communities

Continuing with the analogy of consultants as anthropologists, we may first try to understand the culture of the organization or community with which we are consulting. The notion that a general national or organizational culture such as "the Japanese" or "Apple" exists may disguise more than it reveals. In fact, most organizations, communities, and nations contain multiple component cultures, which overlap and contradict each other. The notion of "trans," as in "transcultural," may better capture the reality of today's world, wherein we all embody customs, values, and allegiances that come from many different groups. For example, when Brooks worked for Sumitomo Metals, Ltd., in Japan, the research and development unit embodied a culture of individuality and eccentricity that stood out as unique against the seeming conformity within the larger organization.

When gathering information about and analyzing an organization's, community's, or group's culture, we might note what they aspire to be or do. We might also try to find out how this aspiration actually works out on the ground, since as Argyris and Schon[5] so aptly point out, we all have "espoused theories," or what we believe and say about ourselves, and "theories in use," or what we actually do. An organization may espouse to outsiders and in their promotional material that they "innovate," but evidence that employees are punished for mistakes may be leading them to conclude that in reality, the organization is unsafe for innovation or risk-taking. For example, in one case study of an organization attempting to transform from a government-regulated to a deregulated industry, one executive described the promotion of an engineer with no human resources experience to vice president of human resources. Even though the organization espoused the value of promotion by merit and diversity, the explanation for the individual's promotion was that the position was too important to trust to someone "we didn't know." In other words, like most of us, we trust those with whom we have a relationship or those who we believe see the world as we do. We trust those we believe are on our side.[6]

Since organizations or communities may see themselves as having certain values, say a community that values "weirdness" such as Portland, Oregon, or Austin, Texas, groups within those communities may identify with the city and appreciate its so-called weirdness, but don't necessarily behave "weirdly" themselves. In organizations, those responsible and educated in finance, sales, engineering, or human resources, for example, are likely to ally and work most easily with others with similar professional training. Especially in an economic environment in which employers are replacing permanent employees with contract workers (or "work for hire" consultants), employees may identify more with others having the same professional training than with their employing organization. Similarly, in international organizations, we might want to find out what values the home office or headquarters holds and how those play out in the field, or how norms of interaction differ among employees from different nations or parts of the world and how the norms of the organization, sector, or profession serve to bring commonality among a nationally varied group.

Several questions can be useful in trying to understand the social and cultural patterns, practices, and logic at work in our client organization or community:

- How do individuals and groups treat hierarchy?
- Who do they consider to be their "in-groups" and "out-groups"? How do they interact with those in their in-groups and out-groups?
- How do they make decisions?

- What "should" statements do we hear from various people? (For example, "We need to be sure and get that in on time" suggests that efficiency and deadlines are important in an organization.)
- Whom do they look up to and how do they behave towards them? Whom do they consider below them and how do they treat those they consider to be below them?
- How do they dress and what does this communicate?
- What is important to them? What do they talk about when not focusing on task?
- How and to whom do they offer information and ideas?
- How do they treat meals and food?
- Where do they get "real work" done?
- What has value to them?

Edgar Schein offers a helpful list of ways that culture can be embedded in an organization, as follows, and these can become rich sources of information for consultants.

- Formal statements of organizational philosophy, mission, vision, values, and materials used for recruiting, selection, and socialization;
- The design of physical space, work environments, and buildings;
- Slogans, language, acronyms, and sayings;
- Deliberate role modeling, training programs, teaching, and coaching by managers and supervisors;
- Explicit rewards, status symbols (e.g., titles), and promotion criteria;
- Stories, legends, or myths about key people and events;
- The organizational activities, processes, or outcomes that leaders pay attention to, measure, and control;
- Leader reactions to critical incidents and organizational crises;
- The workflow and organizational structure;
- Organizational workflow and procedures;
- Organizational goals and the associated criteria used for recruitment, selection, development, promotion, layoffs, and retirement of people.[7]

Schein's work is not only helpful in identifying the current culture, but in determining how a new hoped-for outcome can be brought into the life of the organization or community.

Language and Narratives

One aspect of organizational culture that is sometimes overlooked by consultants and other outsiders is language. Each organization or community has its own unique language based on its history, its industry, and its culture. Especially in large organizations and fields like international development, conversations and written documents can sometimes seem like an alphabet soup because of the proliferation of acronyms and abbreviations. Some words can even be used in ways that are particular to one organization or community, but mean something very different elsewhere. For example, one organization, which was attempting a cultural transformation from a regulated to a deregulated industry, used the word "troublemaker." In this particular context, the word was given the positive meaning of a person who challenged the old ways of doing things and innovated new ones that were more consistent with a deregulated industry.[8]

As consultants, we can easily get lost if we don't learn the language and narratives that circulate in the organization or community. We may also miss important nuances. When we consult in a nation in which the language spoken is not our native tongue, our credibility rises to the extent that we have mastered the local language. Nevertheless, "not knowing" can be a consultant strength if we are genuinely curious and not afraid to ask. If we are engaged in inquiry, generally speaking, no questions are off limits, and the only mistake is to be afraid to ask. For example, Edwards supervised a consulting team that was asked to help market a new exotic type of stone for use in countertops and flooring. The stone was so new that when the team began working on the marketing materials for the company, the stone still didn't have a name. However, well into the process, the client became angry and called the supervisor to say the team was incompetent. In a subsequent follow-up, we discovered that at some point, unbeknownst to the consulting team, the client had named the stone and forgotten to brief the consulting team on the new name. When the team heard the client using the name, they didn't want to seem ignorant, so they didn't ask. The resulting misunderstanding almost derailed the project.

Similarly, the dominant narratives that circulate in organizations and communities can restrict change efforts so that change is only possible when it is congruent with the dominant narrative.[9] This is vividly illustrated in a consultant-led change project in a large Scandinavian company described by Näslund and Pemer.[10] The existing dominant narrative in the company was that it had a strong culture, built on consensus, with substantial employee involvement in decision-making and a leadership style characterized by listening and coaching. The project was to analyze all businesses that were a part of Alpha (the company) according to profitability and growth potential in order to decide which should be retained or discarded. The consultants and project team isolated themselves in a boardroom next to the CEO's office as they went about their work. A story about the perceived "secret" project began to emerge across the organization, which cast the project as a failure because it "wasn't anchored in the organization . . . there was a report that was presented to the board of the company, but then everything turned into chaos. The CEO had to leave after that." The story that circulated about the consultants cast them as incompetent: "'What they tried to do was to milk Alpha for information. They seemed to know less than we did. . . . They suggested measures which were a bit headless, not properly thought through, they hadn't done the accounting' (Vice CEO)" (99). The existing dominant cultural story was adapted to explain why the project failed: no employee involvement, consensus, or listening to employees by the leader. The project team itself characterized the project as good, saying that it wasn't a secret project, and it was consistent with what the company was already doing. The project team's story of the project's failure was that when the project became more widely known in the organization, it "exploded" and turned into "this secret, sensitive project" (100). In this narrative, the consultants were described as being "'impressive' and 'amazing,' working 'three times as hard as regular employees,' and providing Alpha with 'razor sharp' analyses, new information and suggestions for how to improve its business" (100). Nevertheless, the story as told by those outside the project prevailed. When the new CEO arrived, he implemented the solutions recommended by the consultants, but told the organization that "this time, the managers would implement the solutions without the help of external consultants" (97). The challenge for consultants is to know what narratives are important in the organization or community and to pay attention to how the work we are doing fits or doesn't fit with these narratives.

One of the most important but difficult narratives for consultants to name is our own. In the case described here, we might surmise (based on the kinds of narratives most of us bring to our consulting work) that these consultants' narratives might have been, "I am smart and a great analyst. I will solve this client's problem and stop their business decline. I will help them and they will admire what I did and be grateful that I saved them in a way they couldn't do for themselves." This is the expert helper narrative and for the consultants in this story, it was self-sealing. They shut themselves in a room and worked hard to produce a dazzling solution. But because they were so caught up in their own narrative, they couldn't catch the narrative that was forming around them.

From the Future to the Past

How an organization thinks about its future as well as its past is a part of its culture.

- Where does the organization want to go in the future?
- Does the client have a formal vision and mission statement?
- Was the statement created at the top or were all stakeholders involved?
- What is the organization's strategy?
- Is everyone aware of the organization's goals?
- Are the members of the organization aligned on its future?

Of course, different members of any organization may see the answers to questions about the future very differently.

In order to help create the future, we also need to understand the history of an organization.

- Where has the organization been?
- Who founded it?
- What are the critical incidents, crises, and turning points in its history?
- How has the client met previous challenges?
- How successful do members of the organization feel?

By understanding an organization's past, we can gain insight into how it might face the future.

Structure and Processes

While the formal structure of an organization is often diagrammed on an organizational chart, that chart is only one way of grasping how the organization works. Both formal and informal systems and processes are the vehicles by which the people in organizations carry out their work.

Interdependent Systems

A system is a group of connected and interdependent "things." It may be as comprehensive as the universe or as local as the plumbing in our home. Oshry writes that we are all systems creatures: "We exist not in isolation but as integral components of a wide variety of whole human systems—families, organizations, communities, nations, the world."[11] These living systems interact and depend upon natural systems. Indeed, we only begin to feel how interrelated the systems that keep our worlds functioning are when electricity is cut because of a hurricane, city water is rationed because of a regional drought, a plumber isn't available to fix the pipes in the ceiling that flood our house when a severe freeze occurs, or our neighbor's toilet in the apartment upstairs begins to leak into our bedroom.

Organizations and communities have many systems. Among organizations, the internal systems may include communication, human resources, financial, leadership, organizational design, risk management, supply chain, and marketing, for example. Among communities, systems might include transportation, communication, commerce, health, and education, among others.

As consultants, systems-related questions enable us to better understand the dense web of objects and relationships that enable people in organizations and communities to coordinate their efforts toward particular goals. As we try to become more familiar with an organization or community we might try to identify, for example,

- What systems are in place?
- How well are the systems working?
- What is missing compared to other organizations or communities? Is it needed? Why or why not?
- What are people trying to do that is more complex, difficult, dangerous, or convoluted than is necessary because no system exists?

Organizations and communities are also part of and interact or overlap with systems in the environment surrounding them. We might usefully find out:

- What systems connect them to other organizations or communities?
- What systems connect them to the larger world?
- How well do those systems work?
- What systems do they share with others and have an interest in maintaining or improving?
- What systems do other organizations, institutions, communities, associations, or nations control that affect their well-being? How are they working?

As we learn about the systems in our clients' worlds and how they interact with or are co-dependent with our project, we can understand better what our clients face in trying to achieve goals. We can begin to see what we may face as we help them achieve the outcomes they want. Even if our project appears to have a very narrow scope, it will be affected by the systems of the larger organization and/or community, as well as those outside its apparent boundaries. Taking a holistic approach helps us understand how our project fits into larger and dependent systems, and how to utilize that knowledge to achieve our outcomes.

Processes

While we are identifying and analyzing an organization's systems, we can also focus on the processes that may bear on what we're trying to do. Processes are the ways work gets done in organizations. Rummler, Ramias, and Rummler call them "the white space on the organizational chart,"[12] referring to the flow of products, paper, and information between departments. A question for consultants to think about when they come in as outsiders is

- How do things get done around here?

This means we look first at the specific processes that seem to directly bear on the outcome we are seeking.

- What are the specific processes in place that are relevant to our project?
- What are the steps or phases of the processes?
- How well are they working?

As we get deeper into the organization, we might discover that processes we at first thought were completely unrelated to the outcome we are seeking are actually affecting our ability to achieve it.

Process Models

Many models exist for examining work processes, including total quality improvement, reengineering, and six sigma. While these can improve efficiency, they can also be misused. For example, reengineering has sometimes just become a euphemism for downsizing. Similarly, an overemphasis on efficient processes can hurt creativity. After 3M executives adopted a six sigma approach, creativity and innovation in the company actually decreased.[13]

People

People are the heart of organizations and communities. They are potentially both the greatest resource and the biggest obstacle to achieving the outcomes we want. We disregard them at our peril. Our success depends on how well we know the people affected by our project. A readily available source of information regarding the "state of the people" in organizations and communities is their emotions.

The feelings and emotions we see people express—or repress—in an organization or community can tell us a lot about its current condition. Are people angry, frustrated, hopeful, energetic? The most prevalent emotions and feelings can tell us about an organization's or community's readiness to change or grow. The stronger the emotions, the more we can infer that people care about their organization or community. Even if emotions are strongly negative, they carry an energy that may be used to achieve goals. In particular, the passion, pride, and pain people feel in organizations and communities can quickly tell us the challenges we may face and support we can expect among those with whom we are partnering.

Feelings and emotions are particularly important for consultants because they can carry energy, and that energy can potentially be enlisted to help achieve the outcome. By noticing and identifying emotions in client organizations or communities, we can consider how the energy behind them might contribute to (or block) efforts to reach outcomes. Some questions to help us attend to feelings and emotions are the following.

- What are people passionate about?

Passion carries powerful energy that can be put towards accomplishing tasks and goals. Where does that passion lie, and how can we help unleash it for the good of the organization?

- What are people proud of?

Most of us want to be proud of our organization or communities. What are the people in our client organizations or communities proud of? How can that pride be nurtured and expanded?

- Where is the pain?

An organization or community with people in pain is an organization willing to make changes. Following the pain can lead us to core issues. McKnight and Block suggest that sharing sorrows can also help create community.[14] The challenge is not only to recognize and perhaps grieve for the past, but also to find opportunities for the expression of group resilience. The pain may never disappear, but a sense of strength can come from witnessing the stories of each other's experiences and moving forward in new ways.

Where there is passion, pride, and pain, there is human life. And when an organization or community is alive, hope also exists for change and growth.

Power beyond the Organizational Chart

An organization's formal chart of the division of work responsibilities or a community's list of elected officials is only a beginning point for understanding the power and influence that circulates. Anyone in an organization or community can have power and influence. But how that power is distributed, utilized, and communicated varies from organization to organization, community to community, and culture to culture. Questions that can help understand the power dynamics are:

- Who has influence in the organization or community?
- How do they use their influence?
- Who is involved in power struggles?
- Who is engaged in turf wars and what is the turf over which they're struggling?
- Whom do others see as having formal or informal authority?

If we are to achieve the outcomes we're after, we need to understand who has power, how they use their power, and whether they are willing to use it on behalf of the outcome we're after.

In organizations, the CEO and executive team are important players to consider. They may have hired us. We want their support. On the other hand, we can both overestimate and underestimate the power of those at the top of the organization to affect change. A recurring theme in conversations with people in the U.S. at every level of an organization, from CEOs to clerks to mid-level managers, is the limits of their own power to make change. Usually if a positive change could be dictated from the top, it already would have been before consultants arrive on the scene.

Mid-level managers are in the unique position of having a 360-degree view of what's going on in organizations. They interact with both upper management and front-line employees who are doing the operational work of the organization. Sometimes characterized as resistant to change, mid-level managers can also help drive strategic change.[15] Mid-level managers who are centrally networked can use their knowledge and work as boundary spanners to strategically impact change,[16] and thus they can be very helpful to consultants seeking collaborators in the organization.

Many of us overlook the knowledge the support staff has in organizations. If we really want to really understand how the organization works, we can to talk to the support staff. Additionally, members of the support staff have power in their own right. Particularly powerful members of any organization are administrative assistants. They are the gatekeepers to both people and information. They may also talk with administrative assistants to others in the organization and so understand more than those higher up about what is "really" going on in different departments. If we offend a member of this group, we can find ourselves waiting indefinitely for an appointment with a key person or without the important documents we need to proceed. On the other hand, a good administrative assistant who shares information and insights on how to navigate the inner workings of the organization with us can make our work as consultants much easier.

Edwards worked with one administrative assistant in particular who stood out as a consummate professional in her field. She was a "bureaucracy buster." Edwards could tell the assistant what information was needed and before the day was out it was in her hands. She may have encountered a dozen dead ends in her own attempt to acquire the information, but this administrative assistant knew everybody in the organization and "where the bodies were buried." She prevented multiple mistakes as well as saving Edwards countless hours of work. All of us need to find people in our organizations or communities who can help us navigate through them.

Maintenance staff is another group that can wield power in unexpected ways. The maintenance staff can make or break the impression people have of organizations. Being guided through a building that is spotlessly clean tells us a lot about an organization. And so does being led into a conference room that has to be frantically straightened up before an important meeting.

Edwards recalls a maintenance person we will call Seth in a small company in which she had worked. Seth had a quiet authority, which contrasted with that of his supervisor, Jane. Jane, who handled all of the financial matters in the company, took her authority from her boss, the company's founder. She had earned that authority when she discovered a financial error that saved the founder a great deal of money several years ago. From that point on, Jane had her boss's complete confidence. Unfortunately, though, Jane was not an easy person to get along with. She easily flew into tantrums, which terrorized the other employees. She was also vindictive. Anyone who got into a conflict with her could expect to pay for it, literally. Their paycheck might get lost in the mail, or if the check was supposed to be $10,000, it might be missing a zero, and it could take weeks or months to correct the "clerical" error.

One day Jane was scheduled to go to a club luncheon. She had on a new dress, and her hair was meticulously done. Just before she was scheduled to leave, Seth came in to vacuum her office. But the large industrial vacuum cleaner "mysteriously" malfunctioned, and instead of sucking dirt in, it began to spew dirt out. Dirt flew all over the room and all over Jane. She screamed and cursed and yelled at Seth to turn the vacuum off. He kept saying, "Yes, ma'am," but it probably took a good three or four minutes for him to find a way to stop the machine. By that time, dirt was in piles all over the office, on the desk, on her new dress, and in her new hairdo. Seth apologized profusely, but Jane left the building still screaming that now she would have go home and change and was going to be late to her luncheon. As the door slammed behind her, everyone broke out laughing. It was a perfect example of poetic justice.

Power of the Individual

Seth's story is a good example of the informal power anyone in an organization can have. Individual employees can have either positive or negative influence that has little to do with their formal position in the organization. Individual power can derive from several different sources. Questions helpful in understanding how individual power works are:

- Who has knowledge or expertise?
- Who has control over procedures and systems?
- Who has the "right" personality for the context (i.e., extroverted persons are more influential in consulting firms than in engineering departments in a high technology firm)?[17]
- Who has been around the longest?
- What kind of authority does age confer on different people?
- Who has the respect of others (often for being unusually trustworthy, competent, kind, fair, or honest)?
- Who has influence because of whom they know or what they have accomplished, unrelated to the particular organization (the relative of a famous person or a retired but well-known athlete, for example)?

As consultants and as outsiders, we cannot afford to make assumptions about who in the organization or community has the power to be helpful to or to sabotage a project. Understanding power in an organization goes far beyond looking at the official organizational chart of the organization or list of elected and appointed officials in a community.

Relationships and Networks

One robust locus of individual power in organizations and communities is the relationships people form and the networks to which they belong. Relationships and networks are powerful forces in organizations and communities and have the potential to both speed up and block action.

Important questions for consultants to pursue regarding relationships and networks are:

- To what internal and external networks do our project partners belong?
- Which networks in the organization or community are important? Who has meetings with whom? Who has lunch with whom? Who lives in the same parts of town? Who dresses like whom?
- How do these networks function?

Regarding intraorganizational networks, we might ask:

- How are groups within the organization connected?
- What are the natural boundaries between groups?
- Who are the boundary spanners across groups?
- How can boundaries become more permeable?
- How can connections between groups be increased?

We might also look into how the client organization is connected to other organizations:

- What collaborative partnerships are in place or contemplated?
- What mergers, acquisitions, or joint ventures have taken place, or which strategic alliances, partnerships, or consortiums have been formed?
- What opportunities exist to increase interorganizational collaboration?

Tools exist to help with analyzing relationships and networks, from sociograms to sophisticated social network analysis software linked to organizational surveys. Much that is meaningful can be learned and mapped through simple observation and conversations with our partners and others in the organization.[18]

Assets and Gifts

The practice of consulting and giving advice to organizations and communities has historically focused on identifying problems and helping to solve them. We are socialized as professionals to see deficits all around and to view our work as improving people, groups, communities, organizations, and nations by addressing these deficits. The focus on the negative can be demoralizing, energy draining, demeaning, and self-perpetuating. It can also cause us to miss the strengths people in organizations and their communities bring and to overlook their desire to contribute and be a part of something good and bigger than themselves. The assumption that professionals, consultants, politicians, and leaders sometimes bring to organizations, communities, and the world is that they are the only ones with something to contribute. They are the only ones who "know" what "those people," "that organization," or "that community" should do.

In organizations, appreciative inquiry (AI) has reframed change as building on strengths rather than problems and apparent deficits. Appreciative inquiry searches for the best in people, organizations, and the world. It seeks to find what provides the "life" in living systems when they are at their most effective and capable. The questions we ask as appreciative inquirers are intended to strengthen a system's ability to use what is most positive and life giving about it. Thus, "AI interventions focus on the speed of imagination and innovation—instead of the negative, critical, and spiraling diagnoses commonly used in organizations: The discovery, dream, design, and destiny model links the energy of the positive core to changes never thought possible."[19]

When we learn about an organization from an appreciative perspective, we can ask:

- What seems to engage people the most?
- When are they most alive?
- What do people value most about themselves, their work, and their organization?
- What is core to the organization? What gives it life? What, if it were missing, would mean your organization didn't exist?
- If people could see their fondest dreams for themselves and their organization realized, what would that look like?[20]

Questions like these inspire us to focus on the contributions people can make, what they see as a positive future, and what energizes them. The essential question for consultants is:

- What's working and how can we build on that positive energy to create a better future?

A similar transformation from problem to strengths has begun in community development. One of the most powerful and widely adapted approaches to community development over the last decades has been assets-based community development. Pioneered by John Kretzman and John McKnight and the ABCD Institute at Northwestern University, assets-based community development begins with the strengths already existing in communities and then works with those communities to use them to make the community stronger. The central question for exploring communities from this perspective is:

- What assets do communities have that can contribute to building the future they envision for themselves?

Community developers/consultants and their community partners may build an asset map to comprehensively identify a community's strengths. A typical map focuses on five community "pillars": the physical infrastructure and spaces, associations people belong to, institutions that serve people, individuals, and the local economy (Figure 8.1).

Physical resources might include parks, parking areas, and bike paths; associations might include civic events groups, service clubs, and education groups; institutions might include schools and universities, libraries, police and fire departments, and nonprofits; local economy could include for-profits and credit unions; and individuals could include veterans, youth, older adults, activists, and ex-offenders, for example. Each is considered to be not only a member of a community, but a potential contributor to building a community with rich interconnections and in which all would want to live. Appreciative inquiry captures a similar ethos of focusing on strengths and hopes rather than problems.

Whether we're consulting with organizations or communities and whether or not we choose to orient our work toward problems or assets, consultants can usefully ask:

- What gifts do the people in this organization or community have that they may like to contribute to making it better?

This question helps us, as consultants, to recognize what our clients bring to our partnership and to help strengthen the capacity of the organization or community by engaging them in contributing to its development. A related question is:

- How can member gifts be mobilized to help achieve the outcome or goal?

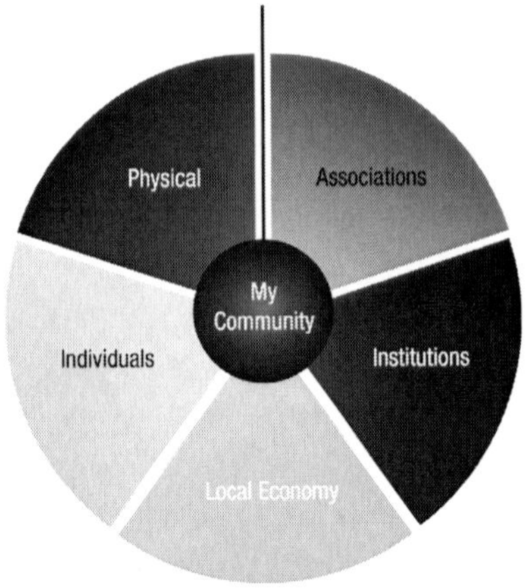

Figure 8.1 Pillars of community

The importance of members' gifts to strengthening the capacities of both organizations and communities is eloquently expressed in the words of John McKnight and Peter Block:

> Citizens create satisfaction by recognizing their individual capacities and skills. We begin to see that the neighborhood is a treasure chest. By opening the chest and putting the gifts together in many different ways, we multiply the power of its riches. A competent community builds on the gifts of its people. It knows that a gift is not a gift until it is given. Before it is given, it is only a beautifully wrapped box in a drawer. It is a capacity held in exile. Gifts need to be named and exchanged. . . .[21]

Consultants can help identify and use the gifts of people that may have gone unrecognized. Helping to find gifts that already exist in organizations and communities and that employees and community members can contribute to successful outcomes may be one of the consultant's greatest gifts to his or her clients.

Conclusion

Entering a client organization or community for consultants is like being a tourist in foreign country. When we are oblivious to the customs and values and ignorant of the ways our hosts communicate, we may believe we are successful sojourners. Were we better informed, sharper observers, or more active learners, we would have a far more accurate and nuanced understanding of the people and nation we are visiting. However, tourists are rarely trying to change the country they are visiting. Consultants step into a world we are being asked to change. The skill with which we undertake that work and whatever success we enjoy will depend on how well we understand the systems we are hoping to change. In the next chapter, we look at tools for systematizing the process of learning about the organization. These are tools that we can use as a solo consultant or with a project team. The data and information we gather are the basis for our analysis of our clients' contexts.

9

Methods of Inquiry

Research is formalized curiosity. It's poking and prodding with purpose.

—Zora Neale Hurston[1]

A boundless, burning curiosity is the most important prerequisite for being good at inquiry. The sincere desire to search for and gather the data and information and develop the knowledge necessary to achieve an outcome is what drives a consulting inquiry. Without the joy of discovery, any method of inquiry becomes just a mechanical exercise. Coming up with answers as a result of an inquiry is like finding buried treasure. But the knowledge produced from even the most brilliant questioning, skillful listening, and creative responses will stay buried if we do not have systematic ways to collect and make sense of what we gather.

Fortunately, a variety of research methods are available to help clients and consultants do the work of inquiry. This chapter lays out some of the many methods and techniques consultants and clients can use to intentionally gather, analyze, and interpret the data and information we find. Each method and technique has strengths and weaknesses and is useful for different purposes.

Planning the Inquiry

Formal and systematic inquiry follows a very logical progression of steps. Without a systematic approach, the trustworthiness and validity of our results are suspect and a shaky foundation on which to base a plan of action.

What Outcome Do We Want?

Without clarity regarding the outcome our client wants, gathering data and information is a waste of our time and our client's resources unless we can state the outcome clearly. When we can state the outcome we are after, formal inquiry provides us with the evidence on which to base the strategies and techniques we will use to get there.

What Do We Need to Know?

Once the outcome statement is clear, the consultant, the consultant team, or the consultant and client team can identify what we need to know in order to develop a strategy and implementation plan for achieving the outcome. For example, if our outcome is the installation of a utilizable electronic data management system for a government agency, then we probably need to know who the stakeholders are. We also will need to find out how they manage the data now and what they need so that the new system fits with the work they need to accomplish. In other words, in the language of research, we need to do a stakeholder needs assessment.

Where Are the Data and Information?

While consultants certainly bring our own knowledge to consulting projects, our existing technical knowledge is rarely enough because we need to contextualize it for particular organizations or communities.

Some of the data and information needed may reside within the organization or community. In large organizations, the HR department, internal consultants such as organizational development specialists, and statisticians may all be helpful to the inquiry team in gathering the data needed. In communities, data and information government agencies may have collected relevant data and information. In very small organizations, the consultant and our contact client may have to assemble the data and information needed.

Important data may be the tacit knowledge the organizational or community members hold. In that case, as in the needs assessment discussed above, we may need to conduct focus groups or interviews to find out what we need to know. Other sources of information and of knowledge are experts from outside organizations who have studied best practices or developed techniques that may inform our deliberations on the best way to achieve the outcome.

Most likely, a variety of data and information sources will contribute to the thinking of the consulting inquiry team as it figures out how to get to the outcome. The consultant has to take an "all of the above" approach to inquiry.

Table 9.1 Organizing data collection

What do we want to know?	*Where are the data located?*	*How will we collect the data?*	*How will we analyze data to come up with findings?*	*What further questions does this raise or action options does it imply?*
Intended outcome: Organizational and training strategies to facilitate and support line workers' learning				
How are new line workers learning their job?	Among the line workers	Interviews with 3 workers on each shift	Identify learning strategies and learning needs and what in the organization facilitates or hinders learning	Questions: Are retired workers available and willing to coach? Action: Pilot an orientation program run by retired workers (What are the pros and cons of this action?)

Organizing the Inquiry

One challenge for consultants, if we are committed to inquiry, is carefully linking the gathering of data, information, and knowledge to what we have determined we need to know to inform any action we decide to take toward achieving the outcome. Why this is challenging is that we often come armed with carefully designed and evaluated data-gathering instruments. But unless those instruments help the team to find out what it needs to know, those instruments are akin to the recurring analogy that if you have a hammer, everything is a nail; if we already have an employee engagement survey we like, it's one misstep to deciding that employee engagement is the issue we need to look into.

One way to avoid this misstep is to construct a way of systematically organizing the links between what we want to know because it is linked to the outcome we're after, and where the data are located and how we will collect and analyze it. The process looks something like this (Table 9.1):

Such organizers serve to focus, organize tasks that need to be done, and share both the structure and the process of the inquiry.

Collecting Data and Information

Various techniques exist for collecting data and information from our clients, including observing them, interviewing and conducting focus groups with them, asking for and going through documents and/or looking at websites, and distributing surveys or questionnaires.

Information gatherers work with two kinds of data: numbers and words. The simple distinction between these is that numbers are most suited to tell us the extent to which something exists and words reveal their qualities. Survey instruments, for example, are an efficient way to find out how prevalent an activity or attitude is among a large group of people. They can easily be distributed electronically and analyzed efficiently. But they do not usually reveal the complexity of human dynamics behind the numbers. And since surveys provide little opportunity for respondents to qualify their responses or even tell us that the questions make no sense in their particular context, the data they provide can be deceiving. On the other hand, interviews and focus groups enable us to see the depth and complexity behind numbers. What are people thinking? What are they actually doing? The downside of interview techniques is that they are time and labor intensive.

Another way of thinking about the information and data we gather is as structured and unstructured. We collect unstructured data "au naturel" from our clients. Collecting unstructured data from our clients enables them to structure their own understanding of their experiences in their organizations or communities. In other words, unstructured data tells us the sense[2] our clients make of their world. Unlike surveys, they do not have to fit their work and lives into predetermined categories. Techniques for gathering these kinds of data are observing the actual organization or community, interviewing the people who work or live there, and collecting relevant print or computer-based information members or outsiders have produced. In contrast, with structured data such as surveys, we prestructure how we want those who complete the data collection instruments to tell us what they know. When we gather data like this, we intend for each person's answers be presented to us in a way that is consistent with how every other person's answers are presented. Each technique has pros and cons. Table 9.2 provides a summary of some of the most common data-gathering techniques.

In the sections that follow, we describe each technique and how consultants can use it in more detail.

Observation

When we are trying to learn more about what is happening in an organization, nothing is more revealing than observing the people and processes in which we are interested. The classic exemplar for doing this kind

Table 9.2 Which data-gathering techniques?

Data	*Technique*	*Pros*	*Cons*
Unstructured	Observation	• direct information on behavior • immediate rather than retrospective	• easy to make inaccurate assumptions about what is observed • time consuming for consultant • can be experienced as intrusive and inconvenient by client • difficult to record • difficult to analyze
	Interviews	• very adaptable • rich source of information • helps build consultant-client relationships	• time consuming for both consultant and client • audio recording or note-taking can be threatening to client
	Print or computer-based information	• unobtrusive • easy to obtain publicly available material	• easy to become overwhelmed by quantity • can be difficult to access and retrieve proprietary information • challenging to analyze and interpret
Structured	Questionnaires	• easily analyzed • efficient with large numbers • comparatively inexpensive	• limited and missing data • may reflect world of consultant more than that of client • poor return rate • survey fatigue
Both	Benchmarking	• allows for social interaction • provides comparison to other organizations	• can be difficult to gain access • challenging to analyze and interpret • data not necessarily transferable

of inquiry is the cultural anthropologist, who lives in another culture in order to understand it. While consultants don't actually live with the clients we work with (although sometimes it starts to feel that way), we do have many opportunities to observe people at work. Observations can be either formal or informal.

When we are in our clients' worlds, we are observing all the time. This may seem self-evident, but as consultants, we are often more focused on our own expertise and assuring our client of its value than we are in learning about our client. For consultants, every meeting, meal in the cafeteria, or walk down the hall provides an opportunity to learn more about our client organization or community and how it works. Even a trip to the restroom can be informative. In their book *Customers for Life*,[3] Carl Sewell and Paul B. Brown write that we can tell a lot about how a business treats its customers just by looking at the restroom. We can also tell a lot about what a community values by observing its public facilities. In a company lavatory, Sewell pays attention not just to the cleanliness, but also to little touches that show attention to detail. Personal touches such as pictures and candles and the presence of stern admonitions about how to dispose of paper products can tell us a lot about an organization. In a similar vein, Oscar Mink, an organizational development consultant, writer, and teacher, pointed out to his consulting students that the best way to know how a consulting gig is going is to listen to what is said in the restroom, not what people say on formal evaluations.[4] The point is that good consultants are always on the alert for anything that gives insight into how the organization or community works.

One seasoned ethnographer, James Spradley, advises that although few of us would admit to being ethnocentric, the beliefs we've developed and the assumptions we make about the way the world works profoundly influence our observations. Enmeshed in our own taken-for-granted ideas about the world, we may assume that love, snow, marriage, worship, work, family, food, death, and many, many other things have basically the same meaning to all human beings. Ethnography begins with the conscious attitude that the ethnographer is almost completely ignorant. We don't know how the people at X organization or in Y community understand their world. As consultants and outsiders, this is what we need to discover.

To make this point, Spradley describes what an Eskimo woman would have to learn if she were trying to understand how the people at Macalester College understand their world:

> [She] would have to begin by learning the language spoken by the students, faculty, and staff. She could stroll the campus paths, sit in classes, and attend special events, but only if she consciously tried to see things from the native point of view would she grasp their perspective. She would need to observe

> and listen to first-year students during their week-long orientation program. She would have to stand in line during registration, listen to students discuss the classes they hoped to get, and visit departments to watch faculty advising students on course selection. She would want to observe secretaries typing, janitors sweeping, and maintenance personnel plowing snow from walks. She would watch the more than 1600 students crowd into the post office area to open their tiny mailboxes, and she would listen to their comments about junk mail and letters from home and no mail at all. She would attend faculty meetings to watch what went on, recording what professors and administrators said and how they behaved. She would sample various courses, attend "keggers" on weekends, read the *Mac Weekly*, and listen by the hour to students discussing things like their "relationships," the "football team," and "work study." She would want to learn the *meanings* of all of these things. She would have to listen to the members of this college community, watch what they did, and participate in their activities to learn such meanings.[5]

Thus, the essential core of ethnography is a concern with the meaning of actions and events to the people we seek to understand. While as consultants we are not conducting a full-fledged ethnography, if we are going to successfully introduce something new into the organization, we must seek to grasp the meaning of actions and events to the people affected. What we pay most attention to depends on the consulting project. For example, when we are studying a fast-food restaurant, our focus may be very different when our aim is to improve customer service than when our aim is to evaluate safety.

Edwards recalls the importance of close observation from a project to improve training for mental health workers in a psychiatric hospital. A psychologist on one of the wards had a good reputation for coaching mental health workers. After interviewing him and several of the workers to learn what he did, what turned out to be the most helpful aspect of the inquiry was observing him on the ward. He stood in the back of the room and never said a word to the workers. But he gave them subtle hand signals. Later, when asked what the hand signals meant, both he and the workers all said that they weren't aware of any hand signals. Yet when shown the signals, both the psychologist and the workers could say what they meant. It seems they had developed a fairly sophisticated nonverbal communication system of which they weren't even aware. On further inquiry, it turned out that the psychologist's father had been a major league baseball player. He had grown up around baseball, and of course hand signals are an integral part of baseball coaching. Observing the hand signals provided a deeper understanding of how the psychologist coached the workers on the ward.

Whether watching others, or even participating ourselves in the everyday life of the organization or community, as consultants we need to monitor the inferences we make about what we see. One way to become more conscious of our inferences is to write down a description of a group of people doing something such as standing in a line or attending a meeting. If we write something like, "Three women are waiting in line with young children. The women are dressed casually, and the children are bored, wiggling and hanging on their mothers," we need to hone our observation skills and take note of the assumptions we make. The word "casual," for example, has different meanings for different groups of people. Are they wearing jeans or short skirts with leggings? As outside observers, we don't know whether the women wearing the clothes believe they are "casual." Similarly, this description assumes that the women are indeed the children's mothers, when in reality, they may be childcare workers or siblings or friends of the children's actual mothers. Similarly, the children may not be bored; they may be tired or have just finished eating a big sugar-laden snack. A description less colored by our own observer assumptions might read,

> Three women waiting in line outside the rec center. Appear to be in their 20s Accompanied by 5 children, 2 boys and 3 girls—seem to be between the ages of about 2–5. One woman has straight blond hair down to her shoulders—is about 5'7". 2 are about 5'4" with dark brown hair, shoulder length—appear to be of Latino background. All three wearing jeans. 2 are wearing grey UMass hoodies; one wearing black spandex sports jacket. . . .

The skill of observing entails picking up details that can inform our understanding of our clients and how they understand their own organizations, communities, work, and lives, while being watchful for the inferences and assumptions we make about them.

Interviews

Interviewing is central to our work as consultants. We interview our clients from the moment of our first contact with them to the very end of our engagement, when we evaluate our work together. Much of this is informal interviewing or learning about how they see the situation, what actions they think may be needed, and how they are responding to our work. Just like our observations, our interviews help us to understand the context within which our expertise needs to fit to be effective. We seek to learn not only about our clients' experiences, hopes, fears, feelings, and understandings of the world they live in, but to learn specific information relevant to our own work in the organization or community. We interview people face to face, by telephone, and increasingly, using various Internet tools. We conduct interviews of both individuals and groups.

Individual Interviews

Some of our individual interviews are informal and ad hoc. Some follow a structured set of questions. Others are semi-structured by topics or issues the interviewer wants to be sure and address, but allow specific questions to evolve as the conversation or interview proceeds. Researchers over the years have developed several simple techniques that can contribute to interviews that elicit important information and insights while demonstrating respect for the person we are interviewing. Box 9.1 provides a list of these techniques.

Box 9.1 Techniques for conducting successful research interviews

Plan the Setting

- Find a quiet place with as few distractions as possible.
- Find a space that is private and where the conversation cannot be overheard.

Establish the Time Frame

- Let the interviewee know how long the interview will last as a sign of respect for the person's time.
- If it seems useful to continue beyond the agreed-upon time, ask at the end of that time if the person is willing to extend the interview, being specific about the length of time.

Prepare the Topics and Possible Questions

- Because clients are busy and we may not have another chance to talk with them, we need to prepare the topics we want to cover and important questions we want to be sure and ask in advance. Clients might also appreciate seeing the questions in advance.

Establish Rapport

- Ask "getting to know you" questions that are easy to answer at the beginning, such as how long they have lived in the community or about the jar of M&Ms on their desk to build rapport. Find a common bond if it seems appropriate.
- Rather than conducting the interview as if it were an oral questionnaire, engage the interviewee in conversation and embed questions within that conversation.

Be Clear about Purpose and Protection

- Tell interviewees the purpose of the interview.
- Tell interviewees how their answers will be used and how their identities will be protected.

Listen

- Spend most of the interview listening instead of talking. Interviewer talk is not very useful data.
- "Stay with" the interviewee. Listen to what he or she is saying rather than planning the next question.

Go Deeper

- Ask interviewees for examples. Most of us are good at talking about our "espoused theories," but concrete illustrations tell us more about what is really going on in the organization and what our interviewee thinks about it.
- Take notes and follow up on what interviewees share.
- Clarify what we don't understand.
- Regularly summarize what our interviewee has said both to make sure we have understood and also to encourage our interviewee to elaborate.

Be Supportive

- Try to enter the interviewees' worlds as they talk.
- Try not to show approval or disapproval of what our interviewee tells us.
- Suspend judgment for the time of the interview. Our job is to gather information rather than draw conclusions.

Bring Closure

- Appreciate the time given and the information shared.
- Ask permission to follow up the conversation if more information is needed later.

Interviews are the most time-consuming technique for gathering and analyzing data. But they are also the best way to learn how our clients make sense of their worlds. Through interviews we can find out about their thoughts and feelings and gather the detailed and complete information that can make our work relevant, on target, and timely. Even just two or three good interviews can jump-start our understanding of our client organization and how things really work.

Group Interviews

Group interviews, compared to individual ones, are an efficient way of gathering information specific to our projects. They also enable us to watch members of our client organization or community interact, and are a way for organization or community members to share information and knowledge with each other, thereby developing group focus on the outcome or project.

Very importantly, group interviews can be a venue for the creation of new knowledge. Since many people learn best in interaction with other people, group interviews can be a powerful way to harness the creativity of a group in one place. Another benefit of a group interview is that it can serve the informational purpose of letting people know what the organization or community is working on.

Group interviews seem to work best when the participants share a characteristic in common relative to the project on which we are working. For example, if we are inquiring into employees' experiences with an IT system, we want to be sure to have people who have had experience with that system. Or if we are helping a school make better use of faculty meetings, interviewing teachers and support staff separately helps to assure each perspective is fully expressed.

Group interviews are most effective when group members are not fearful of each other. Group interviews can be intimidating for many people, particularly when power differentials exist among members, for example when a supervisor and line workers are interviewed in the same group. People tend to defer to the opinions of anyone in a group with a higher ranking in the organization. Similarly, they do not work well when emotions are high or people are afraid to speak freely. Very sensitive issues such as the performance of leaders in an organization are not best explored in an open forum like focus groups.

So why do group interviews work? Referring to one type of group interview, the focus group, Krueger writes,

> The focus group works because it taps into human tendencies.
>
> Attitudes and perceptions relating to concepts, products, services, or programs are developed in part by interaction with other people. We are a product of our environment and are influenced by people around us. . . . People may need to listen to opinions of others before they form their own personal viewpoints.[6]

People generally enjoy the group interview experience. In the hands of a skillful interviewer, participants often find it fun to hear other people's perspectives. They also often find it empowering to have their own views listened to. And again, a group interview can be invaluable to consultants as we help organizations or communities learn about themselves and build new knowledge.

Nevertheless, like individual interviews, conducting group interviews takes planning and coordination. We have to find enough space to accommodate the group and convince people to take the time and go to the inconvenience to participate. Food can often entice potential participants to attend. Most group interviews take about an hour. Many group interviews in organizations are done at lunchtime and in communities in the evenings or on weekends.

Moderating a group interview well requires specific skills. The interviewer needs both good interviewing skills and facilitation skills to manage the conversation and the interpersonal interaction. One relatively easy way to facilitate a group interview is to use a modified nominal group technique. Participants first write down their thoughts on the question being asked. Then the facilitator goes round-robin fashion, giving each person a chance to speak and recording her or his ideas for all to see. The process continues for a round or two until everyone's ideas on a question are exhausted, depending on time, and then the group moves on to the next question. The main benefit of this round-robin format is that it guarantees balanced input from all participants. At the end, ideas can even be prioritized with a multi-voting technique to see how the group weights the ideas they have generated. A second co-facilitator can do the recording so the moderator can focus on the interaction.

When done well, group interviews are a dynamic, energizing experience for everyone involved. And the knowledge generated can jump-start almost any inquiry.

Print or Computer-based Information

Gathering and/or reviewing print or computer-stored information about our client organizations or communities is one of the fastest ways to build an understanding of them. And in a computerized world, vast amounts of information are easily available on even small organizations or communities. This information may be generated internally or externally.

Internally generated information is produced by the organization or community itself, and includes annual reports, a website, Facebook pages, Twitter feeds, newsletters, and marketing materials like brochures or advertisements; it is designed to be read by the public. Other information, particularly in organizations, is intended for internal use. Examples include employee handbooks, policy manuals, training materials, memos, e-mail messages, and internal reports. Externally generated information is produced outside of the organization or community and includes newspaper and magazine articles, library archives, governmental and regulatory reports, customer reviews, books, and blogs. The larger the organization, the more likely a variety of public documents will have been produced.

These kinds of information enable consultants to unobtrusively learn a lot about our clients and without taking up our clients' time. Being informed about our clients enhances their perception of us as consultants who have "done our homework." Through such research, we learn not only "the facts" about our clients, but also the "spin" they put on information in order to create a particular perception of themselves in the outside world. Community and organizational brochures and public websites are a particularly good example of information communicated to project a particular image.

Because computer-based and print information has so proliferated over the past two decades, we can easily get overwhelmed. Like interviews and observations, staying clear regarding why we are gathering it helps guard against getting distracted as we browse. In the first stage of seeking this kind of information, we need to learn about the organization or community prior to the contracting meeting or very early in an assignment so as to have a better grasp of the culture in which we are going to work and more importantly, introduce something new. In the second stage, we are trying to learn about the specific aspect of the organization or community with which we will be working and that we will be trying to change. For example, if we are information systems consultants and have been contracted by a state agency, at first we will want to learn everything we can about the particular agency, including how many employees it has and how many people it serves. If our own work experience is within a business setting, we may want to do a search of recent news stories to understand what particular public pressures or conflicts the agency is facing. We may also find it helpful to read something about what working in a large publicly funded and accountable bureaucracy is like. More specifically to information systems, we will want to gather all we can about the agency's information system from the perspective of the public (if they directly interface with the system) and of course, all of the technical data available within the organization. By understanding what limitations and strains the current system encounters, we can better understand what the system-user interface will need to be.

Questionnaires and Surveys

Structured data are information such as questionnaires and surveys that allow us to structure the answers respondents can give. In other words, respondents must choose from a selection of set responses, which we supply. Controlling in this way what our respondents can tell us allows us to identify broad trends in the organization or community. This form of data collection has the advantage of inexpensively finding out the opinions of a large number of people in a short period of time.

However, the depth of information that can be obtained and the insights afforded are limited. We may also have difficulty getting enough participants to return the completed questionnaire or survey to make them a valid reflection of what is going on in the organization or community. Since computerized survey tools such as SurveyMonkey and Mr. Interview have made the distribution and collection of completed questionnaires and surveys convenient and efficient, their overuse, especially in organizations, has led to survey fatigue for many and cut down on the number of people who are willing to participate.

Since so much readily available information exists on creating and administering questionnaires and surveys, we will not cover the "how to's" here.

Benchmarking

Benchmarking can also be considered a method of inquiry useful to consultants. Stapenhurst (2009) defines benchmarking as "[a] method of measuring and improving organizational performance by comparing ourselves with the best."[7] Searching out organizations that are exemplars of best practices can be very helpful to clients who want to improve their own practices. Benchmarking can be as simple and informal as comparing product prices of competitors to complex formal research projects on very technical processes. Data can be gathered through site visits, databases, reports, and many other sources. Being systematic about which organizations or communities we benchmark and how we manage, analyze, and interpret the data are as important when benchmarking as with any of the other techniques of data collection.

Recording Data

Asking permission to take notes or record when we are observing or interviewing gives people control over their own information. Many researchers prefer to audiotape and later transcribe selected information in order to double-check their perceptions and support our memories of what took place. Videotaping can provide important information about the setting and peoples' body language, but can be intimidating or threatening to them. Sometimes even audiotaping is not feasible if the organization is concerned about proprietary information or employees or community members are fearful of each other or those from outside their own group.

We may be tempted to take the recording and safeguarding of our data for granted. But lost data are often irreplaceable. Again, researchers over the years have developed techniques to help guard against such disasters. Box 9.2 provides a list of some of these techniques.

Box 9.2. Techniques for safe data collection and storage

Keep a Journal

- Keep a daily record of contacts with clients. Try to write down impressions before sleeping on them, and while they are still fresh.
- Particularly with multiple clients, keep track of interactions, impressions, and insights on a routine basis.

Remember Needed Equipment

- Never go anywhere without a pen, pencil, and paper or a small handheld device to take notes on.
- Make a list of equipment needed for meetings or events. Part of feeling confident and communicating that we are competent and can be trusted is having the equipment we need when we arrive at a meeting or event.

Double Check Equipment

- Malfunctioning technology can sabotage the most carefully planned interaction or event. It eats up time and money.
- Make sure our own or the technology provided by the organization, hotel, or event center works as we expect it to.

Have a Plan B

- Have a backup plan in case something doesn't work.
- Expect the unexpected; it almost always happens.

Keep Data Safe

- Make copies immediately after recording data. Assuming an Internet connection (not always the case in remote locations around the world), cloud storage is convenient and readily available across devices.
- Store data copies in a different place than original data.

Managing and Analyzing Unstructured Data

Unstructured data are, well, unstructured; they're messy. The sheer amount can also easily be overwhelming. Experienced researchers begin managing all of this information before they even collect it, constructing organizers like Table 9.1. Part of managing data is deciding how much time we can spend collecting and working with them. If we can only afford to spend fifteen hours on this part of our consulting project, we need to plan to spend part of our time actually interviewing or observing. However, the bulk of our time will end up being devoted to managing, analyzing, and interpreting our data and preparing to communicate or implement the implications of our findings.

An early step in data management is setting up a filing system for storage and from which to work. Software programs such as Atlas.ti and NVivo are useful for this purpose, although file folders are fine. The advantage of software programs is that they not only store and organize data, but aid in analysis. At the same time as we are collecting and organizing our data, we can also reduce the amount on which we will focus. Miles and Huberman[8] explain,

> Data reduction is not something separate from analysis. It is *part* of analysis. The researcher's decisions—which data chunks to code and which to pull out, which evolving story to tell—*are all analytic choices.* Data reduction is a form of analysis that sharpens, sorts, focuses, discards, and organizes data in such a way that "final" conclusions can be drawn and verified.

Because we begin making meaning of our data as soon as we collect them, we can start asking ourselves questions like, "What does it seem to mean?" and "What else do I need to ask?" As Coffey and Atkinson note, "[A]nalysis is not a separate set of procedures applied to an inert body of data."[9] It is instead a "reflexive" activity that takes place throughout the study.

Researchers have developed several methods for analyzing qualitative, unstructured data, some of them very complex. Consultants may use specialized methods for specific purposes, but generally speaking, we are looking for answers to specific questions such as how this particular hospital team can interface with technology with fewer errors, or how that particular police department can improve its relations with a specific community while simultaneously reducing its workforce. This means that we are seeking information that addresses specific questions that pertain to the outcomes we are trying to achieve.

One analytic technique, which also helps to reduce the amount of data we need to analyze, is to first code them according to the questions we want answered. For example, referring to Table 9.1, one code might be, "What strategies do workers use to learn their job?" Once all data that answers this question have been coded, we can sort through these data and analyze the specific strategies that workers reported using. While more complex strategies exist, this is a fairly direct technique for consultants who are looking for immediately practicable results from our data.

Keeping a journal or notes all the way through the project also aids analysis. Our best insights often come when the data are still fresh in our minds, and we remember the details we did not record while actually on site. Writing down our reflections on what we think is important and which questions we need to follow up on will help focus our ongoing contact with our clients and likely inform the recommendations we will eventually make or implement. The key to maintaining clarity throughout the process is to remember the outcome we are trying to reach and collecting and analyzing our data with that outcome always in mind.

As mentioned above, several computer programs exist to help with this process. Although we will not review the specific programs here, all of them enable researchers to (a) upload their data into the software, including media-based as well as transcripts and documents; (b) display the data and provide a way to categorize and code them; (c) enable us to view our data by code once they are coded; (d) look for relationships and frequencies among our data; and (e) display our network of codes as code maps. While software programs do not "make meaning" or interpret our data for us, they help us manage and work with our data in ways that can make our search for meaning in our data more efficient. They also provide an easy interface with the data from surveys and questionnaires.

Interpreting and Checking Our Analysis

What do our data mean and how can we use them to achieve our clients' goals and outcomes? From the moment we decide on the questions we are going to ask, what our data sources will be, what will not be coded as we reduce our data, and the choices we make in analyzing data, we are interpreting the data we've gathered. We are making choices regarding what is important and how we should use the information we've gathered from or about our client.

Since our purpose as consultants is to work with our clients to achieve outcomes, our interpretations generally speak directly to that purpose. However, both language and numbers can have multiple interpretations. The interpretations with which we are most concerned as consultants are those of our clients.

If we are engaging with our clients or a client-team as partners or collaborators, our clients will be engaged in gathering and working with data throughout. This not only assures that the interpretation will be useful, but it provides a measure of trustworthiness or validity to what we find out. The criteria that are most important to assuring trustworthiness are credibility and confirmability.[10]

Credibility means that those we have interviewed, observed, or surveyed believe we have adequately described their reality and experience. Consultant/client teams can raise the credibility of findings by checking with other members of the organization to see if they ring true. Confirmability refers to the extent that another researcher might come to the same conclusions as we did. Consulting teams can increase confirmability by documenting our research procedures and challenging our own findings. Would someone else, say a member of the board of directors, a customer, or a competitor interpret our findings differently? Would the data look different depending on whether we looked at them from an individual, organizational, or community perspective? This critically reflective stance assures that we don't rush prematurely to conclusions. In addition, if our findings suggest a radical change to the organization or community, we can try to corroborate our data by collecting data in different ways from different sources or benchmark our findings and interpretation. We can also avoid doing "hit and run" studies in which we based our understanding of the organization or community on a few quick interviews.

Conclusion

Our trustworthiness as consultants is reflected in the quality of our information-gathering, analysis, interpretation, and recommendations for action. The quality of the outcomes we work together with our clients to achieve depends on solid data and analysis.

Notes

Introduction

1. Andrew Sturdy, "Popular Critiques of Consultancy and a Politics of Management Learning?" *Management Learning* 40, no. 4 (2009): 258–259.
2. John Dewey, "Chapter Eleven: Experience and Thinking," in *Democracy and Education* (New York, NY: The Macmillan Company, 1916).
3. Ann Brooks and Karen Watkins, eds., *The Emerging Power of Action Inquiry Technologies* (San Francisco, CA: Jossey-Bass, 1994); and Peter Reason and Hillary Bradbury, eds., *Handbook of Action Research: Participative Inquiry and Practice* (Thousand Oaks, CA: Sage, 2001).
4. James V. Wertsch, *The Concept of Activity in Soviet Psychology* (Armonk, NY: M.E. Sharpe, 1981).
5. Yrjö Engeström?, Reijo Miettinen, and Raija-Leena Punamäki-Gitai, *Perspectives on Activity Theory* (Cambridge, UK: Cambridge University Press, 1999).
6. Jean Lave and Etienne Wenger, *Situated Learning: Legitimate Peripheral Participation* (Cambridge, UK: Cambridge University Press, 1991).
7. Jean Lave, *Situated Learning: Legitimate Peripheral Participation* (Cambridge, UK: Cambridge University Press, 1991).
8. Edgar Schein, *Process Consultation: Its Role in Organization Development, Volume 1* (New York, NY: Prentice Hall, 1988).
9. John P. Kretzmann and John L. McKnight, *Building Communities from the Inside Out: A Path toward Finding and Mobilizing a Community's Assets* (Chicago, IL: ACTA Publications, 1993).
10. John McKnight and Peter Block, *The Abundant Community: Awakening the Power of Families and Neighborhoods* (San Francisco, CA: Berrett-Koehler, 2010).
11. David L. Cooperrider and Diana Whitney, *Appreciative Inquiry: A Positive Revolution in Change* (San Francisco: Berrett-Koehler, 2005).
12. Michael E. Porter and Mark R. Kramer, "Creating Shared Value: How to Reinvent Capitalism and Unleash a Wave of Innovation," *Harvard Business Review* (2011): 4.
13. Karen Phelan, *I'm Sorry I Broke Your Company* (San Francisco, CA: Berrett-Koehler, 2013), 4–5.

Chapter 1

1. Table includes information from: *Encarta Encyclopedia 2012*; *The American Heritage Dictionary of the English Language*, 5th ed. online, s.v. "consultant," (accessed March 12, 2012), www.ahdictionary.com/; Milan Kubr, ed., *Management Consulting: A Guide to the Profession* (Geneva, Switzerland: International Labour Office, 2002), 10; Linda K. Stroh and Homer H. Johnson, *The Basic Principles of Effective Consulting* (Mahwah, NJ: Lawrence Erlbaum Associates, 2006), 3; Charles J. Fombrun and Daniel F. Oriesek, "The Advice Business: The Industry of Consulting," in *The Advice Business: Essential Tools and Models for Management Consulting* (Upper Saddle River, NJ: Pearson/Prentice-Hall, 2004), 6.

2. Peter Block, *Flawless Consulting: A Guide to Getting Your Expertise Used* (San Francisco, CA: Jossey-Bass/Pfeiffer, 2000), 307.
3. Lewis Pinault, *Consulting Demons: Inside the Unscrupulous World of Global Corporate Consulting* (New York, NY: Harper Collins, 2001).
4. Martin Kuhn, *House of Lies: How Management Consultants Steal Your Watch and Then Tell You the Time* (New York, NY: Warner Business Books, 2005).
5. Elaine Biech, *The Business of Consulting: The Basics and Beyond*, 2nd ed. (San Francisco: Pfeiffer/John Wiley and Sons, 2007), 16–17. (Interstate Highway 495 surrounds the U.S. capital of Washington, D.C., and its immediate suburbs. The term "beltway" is frequently incorporated into phrases that refer to American government or politics.)
6. Maribeth Buchanan, account manager, Kennedy Consulting Research & Advisory, Kennedy Information, LLC, personal communication.
7. James R. Warren, "Predicting and Enhancing Client Success," in *Creative Consulting*, ed. Anthony E. Buono (Greenwich, CT: Information Age Publishing, 2004), 345–370.
8. David H. Maister, Charles H. Green, and Robert M. Galford, *The Trusted Advisor* (New York, NY: Free Press, 2000).
9. William Alger, in Kubr, *Management Consulting*, 6.
10. Ann K. Brooks, unpublished research (2008).
11. Robert Kegan, *In Over Our Heads: The Mental Demands of Modern Life* (Cambridge, MA: Harvard University Press, 1994).
12. Robert Schaffer, *High Impact Consulting: How Clients and Consultants Can Work Together to Achieve Extraordinary Results,* 2nd ed. (San Francisco, CA: Jossey-Bass, 2002), 3.
13. Bill Saporito, "The Conspiracy to End Cancer," *Time Magazine*, April 2013, http://healthland.time.com/2013/04/01/the-conspiracy-to-end-cancer/.
14. Ian Graham, "The Compleat Requirements Analyst," *IEEE Software* 20, no. 6, (2003): 100.
15. Ibid.
16. Mary Hennock, "News Analysis: China Looks to Western Partners to Reshape Its Universities," *The Chronicle of Higher Education*, July 17, 2011. http://chronicle.com.libproxy.txstate.edu/article/News-Analysis-China-Looks-to/128222/.
17. Leana Wen and Joshua Kosowski, *When Doctors Don't Listen: How to Avoid Misdiagnoses and Unnecessary Tests* (New York: St Martins Press, 2013), 8.
18. Ariel Le, "Interview with a Consultant," MAN 328, McCombs School of Business, University of Texas at Austin, February 2013.

Chapter 2

1. John Dewey, *Logic—The Theory of Inquiry* (New York: Henry Holt and Co. 1938), 460.
2. Peter Block, *Flawless Consulting: A Guide to Getting Your Expertise Used*, 3rd ed. (San Francisco: Pfeiffer/John Wiley and Sons, 2011), 6–9.
3. Eric L. Trist and Kenneth W. Bamforth, "Some Social and Psychological Consequences of the Longwall Method of Coal Getting: An Examination of the Psychological Situation and Defences of a Work Group in Relation to the Social Structure and Technological Content of the Work System," *Human Relations* 4, no. 3 (1951): 3–38.
4. Reynaldo G. Lozano, "A Socio-technical Analysis of Knowledgeable Practice in Radiation Therapy" (Ph.D. dissertation, Texas State University, 2012).
5. Walt Bogdanich, "The Radiation Boom: As Technology Surges, Radiation Safeguards Lag," *The New York Times*, January 26, 2010, http://www.nytimes.com/2010/01/27/us/27radiation.html?pagewanted = all&_r = 0.
6. Matt Kouri, interview with coauthor, June 1, 2010.
7. Edgar H. Schein, "The Concept of Client from a Process Consultation Perspective: A Guide for Change Agents," working paper #3946, March 1997.
8. Anita Williams Woolley, Christopher F. Chabris, Alex Pentland, Nada Hashmi, and Thomas W. Malone, "Evidence for a Collective Intelligence Factor in the Performance of Human Groups," *Science* 330, no. 6004 (2010): 686–688.

9. Lynda Gratton and Tamara J. Erickson, "Eight Ways to Build Collaborative Teams," in *Harvard Business Review on Collaborating Effectively* (Boston: Harvard Business School Publishing Corporation, 2011), 50.
10. John P. Kretzmann and John L. McKnight, *Building Communities from the Inside Out: A Path toward Mobilizing a Community's Assets* (Chicago: ACTA Publications, 1993).
11. Ann K. Brooks and Paul Kavanaugh, "Empowering the Surrounding Community," in *High-Performing Hispanic Schools: Creating Learning Communities*, eds. Pedro Reyes, Jay D. Scribner, and Alicia Paredes Scribner (New York: Teachers College Press, 1999), 61–93.
12. Elba Williams, "The Perspectives of Latina Immigrant Mothers of Children in the Public Schools, (unpublished data, Texas State University, 2012).
13. Jennifer Martineau and Kelly Hannum, Evaluating the Impact of Leadership Development: A Professional Guide (Greensboro, NC: Center for Creative Leadership, Greensboro, NC, 2001), 9.
14. Reg Revans, *ABC of Action Learning* (London: Gower, 2011).
15. Kurt Lewin, *Resolving Social Conflicts: Selected Papers on Group Dynamics*, ed. Gertrude W. Lewin (New York: Harper and Row, 1948).
16. Frank Leistner, *Mastering Organizational Knowledge Flow: How to Make Knowledge Sharing Work* (Hoboken: Wiley and SAS, 2010).
17. Dwight D. Eisenhower, "Remarks" (National Defense Executive Reserve Conference, Washington, DC, November 14, 1957). http://www.presidency.ucsb.edu/ws/?pid=10951
18. Helen Gadsden-Ross, "Knowledge Deficit: What's the Effect on the New Employee?" (Ph.D. diss. proposal, Texas State University, 2012).
19. Michael Scriven, *Evaluation Thesaurus* (Thousand Oaks: Sage, 1991), 169.
20. Frank Leistner, *Mastering Organizational Knowledge Flow: How to Make Knowledge Sharing Work* (Hoboken: Wiley and SAS, 2010).

Chapter 3

1. Carol Schaefer, *Grandmothers Counsel the World: Women Elders Offer Their Vision for Our Planet* (Boston, MA: Trumpeter Press, 2006), 19.
2. Edgar H. Schein, Adam Kahane, and Adam Scharmer, "Humility and Ignorance: What It Takes to Be an Effective Process Consultant," *Reflections* 3, no. 2 (2001): 10.
3. Ibid.
4. Thomas S. Eliot, *Shakespeare and the Stoicism of Seneca*. (London, UK: Oxford University Press, 1927), 8.
5. Robert C. Solomon, *A Better Way to Think about Business* (New York: Oxford University Press, 1999), 70.
6. Dusya Vera and Antonio Rodriguez-Lopez, "Strategic Virtues: Humility as a Source of Competitive Advantage," *Organizational Dynamics* 33, no. 4 (2004): 394.
7. Christopher Peterson and Martin Seligman, *Character Strengths and Virtues: A Handbook and Classification* (New York, NY: Oxford University Press, 2004).
8. Jim Collins, "Level 5 Leadership: The Triumph of Humility and Fierce Resolve," *Harvard Business Review* 83, no. 7/8 (2001): 67–77.
9. Dusya Vera and Antonio Rodriguez-Lopez, *Organizational Dynamics* 33, no. 4 (2004): 393–408.
10. June P. Tangney, "Humility," in *Handbook of Positive Psychology*, ed. C. R. Snyder and Shane J. Lopez (New York: Oxford University Press, 2002), 413; June P. Tangney, "Humility: Theoretical Perspectives, Empirical Findings and Directions for Future Research," *Journal of Social and Clinical Psychology* 19, no. 1 (2000): 70–82.
11. David G. Myers and Jack Ridl, "Can We All Be Better Than Average?" *Psychology Today* (August 1979): 89. Cited in Tangney, 413.
12. Tom Pyszczynski et al., "Why Do People Need Self-Esteem? A Theoretical and Empirical Review," *Psychological Bulletin* 130, no. 3 (2004): 435–468.
13. Mark R. Leary and Roy F. Baumeister, "The Nature and Function of Self-Esteem: Sociometer Theory," in Advances in Experimental Social Psychology, ed. Mark P. Zanna (New York, NY: Academic Press, 2000), 32.

14. Ess, Charles, "Liberal Arts and Distance Education: Can Socratic Virtue (*arete*) and Confucius' Exemplary Person (*junzi*) Be Taught Online?," in *Brave New Classrooms: Educational Democracy and the Internet*, ed. Mark Pegrum and Joe Lockard (New York: Peter Lang, 2007), 192.
15. Robert K. Greenleaf, *Servant Leadership: A Journey into the Nature of Legitimate Power and Greatness* (Mahwah, NJ: Paulist Press, 2002), 354.
16. Christopher Peterson and Martin Seligman, *Character Strengths and Virtues*, 472.
17. Ibid., 473–474.
18. W. Keith Campbell et al., "Among Friends? An Examination of Friendship and the Self-Serving Bias," *British Journal of Social Psychology* 30 (2000): 229–239.
19. Dianne M. Tice et al., "When Modesty Prevails: Differential Favorability of Self-Presentation to Friends and Strangers," *Journal of Personality and Social Psychology* 69 (1995): 1120–1138.
20. Ellen J. Langer and Mihnea Moldoveanu, "Mindfulness Research and the Future," *Journal of Social Issues* 56, no. 1 (2000): 129–139.
21. Ibid.
22. Ibid.
23. Ibid.
24. Thanissaro Bhikkhu, "The Path of Concentration & Mindfulness," *Access to Insight* 8 (March 2011), accessed March 12 2012, http://www.accesstoinsight.org/lib/authors/thanissaro/concmind.html.
25. Goenka, S.N. "The Art of Living: Vipassana Meditation," *Vipassana Meditation Website*, http://www.dhamma.org/en/art.shtml.
26. Rian Hetherington, *Realizing Change: Vipassana Meditation in Action* (Seattle, WA: Pariyatti Press, 2003): 179.
27. Ellen J. Langer and Mihnea Moldoveanu, "The Construct of Mindfulness," *Journal of Social Issues* 56, no. 1 (2000): 1–9; and Daniel Goleman, *Destructive Emotions: How Can We Overcome Them?: A Scientific Dialogue with the Dalai Lama, Narrated by Daniel Goleman* (New York: Bantam, 2004).
28. Karl E. Weick and Ted Putnam, "Organizing for Mindfulness: Eastern Wisdom and Western Knowledge," *Journal of Management Inquiry* 15, no. 3 (2006): 286.
29. Karen E. Klein, "Smart Answers: Why Self-Employed Consultants Fail," *Bloomberg Businessweek: Small Business*, May 10, 2011, http://www.businessweek.com/smallbiz/content/may2011/sb2011059_763239.html.
30. Kristin D. Neff and Roos Vonk, "Self-Compassion versus Global Self-Esteem: Two Different Ways of Relating to Oneself," *Journal of Personality* 77, no. 1 (2009): 23–50.
31. Kristin D. Neff, "Self-Compassion: An Alternative Conceptualization of a Healthy Attitude Toward Oneself," *Self and Identity* 2 (2003): 85–102.
32. Kristin D. Neff, "Development and Validation of a Scale to Measure Self-Compassion," *Self and Identity* 2 (2003): 223–250.
33. John Donne, *The Works of John Donne, Vol. III*, ed. Henry Alford (London, UK: John W. Parker, 1839) 574–575.
34. Eric Klinenberg, "Denaturalizing Disaster: A Social Autopsy of the 1995 Chicago Heat Wave," *Theory and Society* 28 (1999) 239–295.
35. Peter Dreier, "Katrina and Power in America," *Urban Affairs Review*, 41. No. 4 (2006): 528–549.
36. Ted Schrecker, "Denaturalizing Scarcity: A Strategy of Enquiry for Public-Health Ethics," *Bulletin of the World Health Organization* 86, no. 8 (August 2008).
37. Michael E. Porter and Mark R. Kramer, "Creating Shared Value," *Harvard Business Review* (January–February 2011): 65.
38. Ibid.
39. David L. Cooperrider, "Appreciative Inquiry: Toward a Methodology for Understanding and Enhancing Organizational Innovation," (Ph.D. dissertation, Case Western Reserve University, 1986).
40. John McKnight and Peter Block, *The Abundant Community: Awakening the Power of Families and Neighborhoods* (San Francisco, CA: Berrett-Kohler, 2012).

PII-Intro

1. Milan Kubr and Martin Kubr, eds., *Management Consulting: A Guide to the Profession* (Geneva, Switzerland: International Labour Office, 2002), 61.
2. Ibid., 67.

Chapter 4

1. Maya Angelou, *Oprah Winfrey Show*, October 3, 2008.
2. Peter Block, *Flawless Consulting: A Guide to Getting Your Expertise Used* (San Francisco, CA: Jossey-Bass/Pfeiffer, 2000).
3. Karen Phelan, *I'm Sorry I Broke Your Company* (San Francisco: Berrett-Koehler, 2013).
4. Stephen Fineman, ed., *The Emotional Organization: Passions and Power* (Oxford, UK: Blackwell Publishing, 2008), 218.
5. Craig C. Lundberg and Cheri A. Young, "A Note on Emotions and Consultancy," *Journal of Organizational Change Management* 14, no. 6 (2001): 530.
6. Carroll E. Izard, "Emotion Theory and Research: Highlights, Unanswered Questions, and Emerging Issues," *Annual Review of Psychology* 60 (2009): 1–25.
7. Louis Cozolino, *The Neuroscience of Human Relationships: Attachment and the Developing Social Brain* (New York, NY: W.W. Norton & Co., 2006), 10.
8. Norbert Schwartz, "Feelings-as-Information Theory," in *Handbook of Theories of Social Psychology: Volume One*, ed. Paul A. M. Van Lange, et al. (Thousand Oaks, CA: Sage, 2011), 289–308.
9. Donald A. Redlmeier and Simon D. Baxter, "Rainy Weather and Medical School Admission Interviews," *Canadian Medical Association Journal* 181 (2009): 933.
10. David Hirshleifer and Tyler Shumway, "Good Day Sunshine: Stock Market Returns and the Weather," *Journal of Finance* 58 (2003): 1009–1032.
11. Jennifer S. Lerner et al, "Effects of Fear and Anger on Perceived Risks of Terrorism: A National Field Experiment," *Psychological Science* 14 (2003): 144–150.
12. Jennifer S. Lerner, Deborah A. Small, and George Loewenstein, "Heart Strings and Purse Strings: Carryover Effects of Emotions on Economic Decisions," Psychological Science 15, no. 5 (May 2004): 337–341.
13. Drew Westen et al., "Neural Bases of Motivated Reasoning: An FMRI Study of Emotional Constraints on Partisan Political Judgment in the 2004 U.S. Presidential Election," *Journal of Cognitive Neuroscience* 18, no. 1 (2006): 1947–1958.
14. Tina Kiefer, "Feeling Bad: Antecedents and Consequences of Negative Emotions in Ongoing Change," *Organizational Behavior* 26, no. 8 (2005): 875–897.
15. Srinivasan S. Pillay, *Your Brain and Business: The Neuroscience of Great Leaders* (Upper Saddle River, NJ: Pearson Education/FT Press, 2011).
16. Ibid., 122.
17. Ibid., 126.
18. Ibid., 128.
19. S. Douglas Pugh, "Service with a Smile: Emotional Contagion in the Service Encounter," *Academy of Management Journal* 44, no. 5 (2001): 1018–1027.
20. Elaine Hatfield, John T. Cacioppo, and Richard L. Rapson, *Emotional Contagion* (New York, NY: Cambridge University Press, 1994).
21. Jonathan D. Cohen, "The Vulcanization of the Human Brain: A Neural Perspective on Interactions between Cognition and Emotion," *Journal of Economic Perspectives* 19, no. 40 (2005): 3–24.
22. Todd F. Heatherton, "Neuroscience of Self and Self-regulation," *Annual Review of Psychology* 62 (2011): 363–390.
23. Edgar Schein, *Helping: How to Offer, Give, and Receive Help* (San Francisco: Berrett-Kohler, 2009), 147.
24. Helen Reiss, "Commentary | Empathy in Medicine—A Neurobiological Perspective," *Journal of the American Medical Association* 304, no. 14: 1604–1605.
25. Karen Phelan, *I'm Sorry I Broke Your Company* (San Francisco: Berrett-Koehler, 2013).

26. Ibid., 97.
27. Daniel J. Siegel, *The Developing Mind: How Relationships and the Brain Interact to Shape Who We Are* (New York, NY: Guilford Press, 1999).
28. Karen Phelan, *I'm Sorry I Broke Your Company* (San Francisco: Berrett-Koehler, 2013), 99.
29. Jamil Zaki and Kevin Ochsner, "The Neuroscience of Empathy: Progress, Pitfalls and Promise," *Nature Neuroscience* 15 (2012): 675–680.
30. Jamil Zaki, Jochen Weber, Niall Bolger, and Kevin Ochsner, "The Neural Bases of Empathic Accuracy," *Proceedings of the National Academy of Science of the USA* 106, no. 27 (2009): 11382–11387.
31. Helen Reiss et al., "Empathy Training for Resident Physicians: A Randomized Controlled Trial of a Neuroscience-Informed Curriculum," *Journal of General Internal Medicine* 26, no. 10 (2011): 1280–1286.
32. Helen Riess, "Empathy in Medicine—A Neurobiological Perspective," *JAMA* 304, no. 14 (2010): 1604–1605.
33. Dev Patnaik, "Viewpoint: Empathy Is Growth, *Bloomberg Business: Innovation and Design*, March 4, 2009, *http://www.businessweek.com/innovate/content/mar2009/id2009034_766385.htm*.
34. Peter Block, *Flawless Consulting: A Guide to Getting Your Expertise Used* (San Francisco, CA: Wiley & Sons, 2000), 37.
35. Ralph Adolphs, "Trust in the Brain," *Nature Neuroscience* 5, no. 3 (2002): 192–193.
36. Edgar Schein, *Helping: How to Offer, Give, and Receive Help: Understanding Effective Dynamics in One-to-One, Group, and Organizational Relationships* (San Francisco: Berrett-Kohler, 2009), 147.
37. Stephen Fineman, *The Emotional Organization: Passions and Power* (San Francisco, CA: John Wiley & Sons, 2008), 1.
38. Ibid., 3.

Chapter 5

1. Mats Alvesson, "Knowledge Work: Ambiguity, Image and Identity," *Human Relations* 54, no. 7 (2001): 863–886.
2. Lynne Gilfillan, Ph.D., personal correspondence with coauthor, March 21, 2013.
3. Edgar H. Schein, *Helping: How to Offer, Give, and Receive Help* (San Francisco: Berrett-Koehler, 2009), 33.
4. Thomas L. Friedman, "Collaborate vs. Collaborate," *The New York Times*, January 12, 2013, http://www.nytimes.com/2013/01/13/opinion/sunday/friedman-collaborate-vs-collaborate.html?_r=0
5. Dan Sanker, *Collaborate: The Art of We* (Hoboken, NJ: John Wiley, 2012), 3.
6. Keith Merron, *Consulting Mastery: How the Best Make the Biggest Difference* (San Francisco, CA: Berrett-Koehler, 2005), 39.
7. Namisha Kachhla, presentation in Edwards's MAN 328 Consulting and Change Management class at the McCombs School of Business, University of Texas at Austin, Austin, TX, January 29, 2013.
8. Moon Ihlwan, "Camp Samsung," *BusinessWeek*, July 3, 2006, 46.
9. Carol C. Gilligan, *In a Different Voice* (Cambridge, MA: Harvard University Press, 1982).
10. Edgar Schein, *Process Consultation Revisited: Building the Helping Relationship* (Reading, MA: Addison-Wesley, 1999), 6.
11. Euripides, *The Bacchae*, quoted in *Fearless Consulting: Temptations, Risks and Limits of the Profession* by Erik de Haan (Chichester, West Sussex, UK: John Wiley & Sons, 2006), 7.
12. Erik de Haan, *Fearless Consulting: Temptations, Risks and Limits of the Profession* (Chichester, West Sussex, UK: John Wiley & Sons, 2006), 5.
13. Edgar Schein, *Process Consultation Revisited: Building the Helping Relationship* (Reading, MA: Addison-Wesley, 1999), 55.
14. Linda Donelson, interview with coauthor, 2010.

15. David H. Maister, Charles H. Green, and Robert M. Galford, *The Trusted Advisor* (New York: Free Press, 2000), 69.
16. Jean-Philippe Barrett, Lisa Feldman Laurenceau, and Paula R. Pietromonaco, "Intimacy as an Interpersonal Process: The Importance of Self-disclosure, Partner Disclosure, and Perceived Partner Responsiveness in Interpersonal Exchanges," *Journal of Personality and Social Psychology* 74, no. 5 (1998): 1238–1251.
17. David H. Maister, Charles H. Green, and Robert M. Galford, *The Trusted Advisor* (New York: Free Press, 2000), 80.
18. Leigh L. Thompson, *The Mind and Heart of the Negotiator*, 5th ed. (Upper Saddle River, NJ: Pearson Education, 2012), 139–142.
19. Daniel Kahneman, "Maps of Bounded Rationality: A Perspective on Intuitive Judgment and Choice," Nobel Prize Lecture, Aula Magna, Stockholm University, Stockholm, Sweden, December 8, 2002.
20. Michael Polanyi, *The Tacit Dimension* (Chicago, IL: University of Chicago Press, 1966); Donald Schon, *The Reflective Practitioner: How Professionals Think in Action* (New York: Basic Books, 1983); and Ikujiro Nonaka and Tokyo Hirotaka, *The Knowledge-creating Company: How Japanese Companies Create the Dynamics of Innovation* (New York, NY: Oxford University Press, 1995).
21. Edward Salas, Michael A. Rosen, and Deborah DiazGranados, "Expertise-Based Intuition and Decision Making in Organizations," *Journal of Management* 36, no. 4 (2010): 941–973.
22. Keith E. Stanovich and Richard F. West, "Individual Differences in Reasoning: Implications for the Rationality Debate," *Behavioral and Brain Sciences* 23, no. 5 (2000): 645–726.
23. Raanan Lipshitz, Gary Klein, Judith Orasanu, and Edward Salas, "Taking Stock of Naturalistic Decision Making," *Journal of Behavioral Decision Making* 14, no. 5 (2001): 331–352.
24. Amy Edmondson, "Psychological Safety and Learning Behavior in Work Teams," *Administrative Science Quarterly* 44, no. 2 (1999): 350–383.
25. Ann Brooks, "Power and the Production of Knowledge: Collective Team Learning in Work Organizations," *Human Resource Development Quarterly* 5, no. 4 (1994): 213–235.
26. Amy Edmondson, "Psychological Safety and Learning Behavior in Work Teams," *Administrative Science Quarterly* 44, no. 2 (1999): 375.
27. Edgar H. Schein, *Helping: How to Offer, Give, and Receive Help* (San Francisco: Berrett-Koehler, 2009), 33.
28. Mirela Schwarz and Timothy Clark, "Clients' Different Moves in Managing the Client-Consultant Relationship," in *Client-Consultant Collaboration: Coping with Complexity and Change*, ed. Anthony F. Buono and Flemming Poulfelt, 3–28, (Charlotte, NC: Information Age Publishing, 2009), 16.
29. Tim Garippa, interview with coauthor, January 31, 2012.
30. Elizabeth Haas Edersheim, *McKinsey's Marvin Bower: Vision, Leadership & the Creation of Management Consulting* (Hoboken, NJ: John Wiley & Sons, 2004).

Chapter 6

1. Dave Eggers, *A Hologram for the King* (San Francisco, CA: McSweeney's, 2012), 22.
2. Peter Sorensen et al., "Consulting in the Middle East: Recent Experiences and Alternative Models," (paper presented at the Professional Development Workshop, Academy of Management, Boston, MA, August 3–7, 2012).
3. Milan Kubr, ed., *Management Consulting: A Guide to the Profession* (Geneva, CH: International Labor Office, 2002), 115; and Barry Curnow and Jonathan Reuvid, *International Guide to Management Consultancy: The Evolution, Practice and Structure of Management Consultancy Worldwide*, 2nd ed. (London, UK: Kogan Page, 2006).
4. Society for Intercultural Exchange, Training, and Research, http://www.sietar.org.uk/; and Penelope Cagney, *Nonprofit Consulting Essentials: What Nonprofits and Consultants Need to Know* (Hoboken, NJ: John Wiley & Sons, Inc., 2010).
5. Milan Kubr, ed., *Management Consulting: A Guide to the Profession* (Geneva, CH: International Labor Office, 2002), 114.

6. Geert Hofstede, *Culture's Consequences: International Differences in Work-related Values* (Beverly Hills, CA: Sage, 1980), 43.
7. Jeanne Brett, Kristin Behfar, and Mary C. Kern, "Managing Multicultural Teams," *Harvard Business Review* (November 2006): 86.
8. John Alston and Isao Takei, *Japanese Business Culture and Practices: A Guide to Twenty-First Century Japanese Business* (Lincoln, NE: iUniverse, 2005), 5.
9. Geert Hofstede, Gert Jan Hofstede, and Michael Minkov, *Cultures and Organizations: Software for the Mind*, 3rd ed. (New York, NY: McGraw-Hill, 2010).
10. Professor Emeritus Geert Hofstede, "Countries-United States-China," http://www.geert-hofstede.com.
11. Cornelius N. Grove, Grovewell Global Leadership Solutions LLC, "Introduction to the GLOBE Research Project on Leadership Worldwide" (2005), http://www.grovewell.com/pub-GLOBE-intro.html.
12. Ying Zhu et al., "Neural Basis of Cultural Influence on Self-Representation," *NeuroImage* 34, no. 3 (2007): 1310–1316.
13. Charles Hampden-Turner and Fons Trompenaars, *Riding the Waves of Culture: Understanding Diversity in Global Business* (New York, NY: McGraw-Hill, 1997).
14. Brendan McSweeney, "Hofstede's Model of National Cultural Differences and Consequences: A Triumph of Faith—A Failure of Analysis," *Human Relations* 55, no. 1 (2002): 89–118.
15. "The term 'mashup' . . . was originally used to describe songs that meshed two different styles of music into one song. For example, a classic rock song put to a well-known hip-hop beat may be considered a mashup. It is also used to describe videos that have been compiled using different clips from multiple sources. For example, a skateboarding movie created from several different skateboard videos found would be considered a video mashup. A mashup also describes a Web application that combines multiple services into a single application." See http://www.techterms.com/definition/mashup.
16. Penelope Cagney, *Nonprofit Consulting Essentials: What Nonprofits and Consultants Need to Know* (Hoboken, NJ: John Wiley & Sons, Inc., 2010), 70.
17. Victor J. Friedman and Ariane Berthoin Antal, "Negotiating Reality: A Theory of Action Approach to Intercultural Competence," *Management Learning* 36, no. 1 (2005): 70.
18. Ibid., 77.
19. Todd F. Heatherton, "Neuroscience of Self and Self-Regulation," *Annual Review of Psychology* 62 (2011): 363–390, doi: 10.1146/annurev.psych.121208.131616.
20. Ibid., 366.
21. Jeanne Brett, Kristin Behfar, and Mary C. Kern, "Managing Multicultural Teams," *Harvard Business Review* 84, no. 11 (2006): 84–91.
22. Ying Hong et al., "Multicultural Minds: A Dynamic Constructivist Approach to Culture and Cognition," *American Psychologist* 55, no. 7 (2000): 709–720.
23. Jawaharlal Nehru, *Visit to America* (New York, NY: J. Day Co., 1950), 59.

Chapter 7

1. Personal communication with the university vice president, August 2011.
2. Mary F. Belenky et al., *Women's Ways of Knowing: The Development of Self, Voice, and Mind* (New York: Basic Books, 1986).
3. Michael H. Hoppe and the Center for Creative Leadership, *Active Listening: Improve Your Ability to Listen and Lead* (San Francisco: Pfeiffer, 2011).
4. Merriam Webster, 11th ed., s.v. "medical attention, in the online version," http://www.merriam-webster.com/medical/attention (accessed June 10, 2012).
5. Amishi P. Jha, Jason Krompinger, and Michael J. Baime, "Mindfulness Training Modifies Subsystems of Attention," *Cognitive Affective Behavioral Neuroscience* 7, no. 2 (2007): 109–119.
6. Jim Collins, *Good to Great: Why Some Companies Make the Leap. . .and Others Don't* (New York: Harper Collins, 2001).
7. Michael Marquardt, *Leading with Questions: How Leaders Find the Right Solutions by Knowing What to Ask* (San Francisco, CA: Jossey-Bass, 2005), 80.

8. Albert Einstein, *The Ultimate Quotable Einstein*, ed. Alice Calaprice (Princeton, NJ: Princeton University Press and the Hebrew University of Jerusalem, 2011), 425.
9. Reg Revans, *The ABC of Action Learning* (Surrey, UK: Gower, 2011).
10. Albert E. Barker, "Remembering Reg Revans: Action Learning's Principal Pioneer," in *Action Learning: History and Evolution* by Yury Boshyk and Robert Dilworth (Basingstoke, Hampshire, UK: Palgrave Macmillan, 2010), 34.
11. Yury Boshyk and Robert Dilworth, *Action Learning: History and Evolution* (Basingstoke, Hampshire, UK: Palgrave Macmillan, 2010), 34.
12. Judy O'Neil and Victoria Marsick, *Understanding Action Learning* (Washington, D.C.: AOM, 2007), 82.
13. Michael Gibbons et al., *The New Production of Knowledge: The Dynamics of Science and Research in Contemporary Societies* (London: Sage, 1994).
14. Daryl Allan Michel, "An Analysis of Faculty Meeting Content and Processes: A Multi-case Study of Three South Texas Schools," (Ph.D. dissertation, Texas State University, 2011).
15. Ann K. Brooks, "Power and the Production of Knowledge: Collective Team Learning in Work Organizations," *Human Resource Development Quarterly* 5, no. 3 (1994): 221.
16. Amy C. Edmondson, "Managing the Risk of Learning: Psychological Safety in Work Teams," in *International Handbook of Organizational Teamwork and Cooperative Working*, ed. Dean Tjosvold, Michael A. West, and Ken G. Smith (Hoboken, NJ: Wiley, 2003), 255–276.
17. Stuart MacDonald, "Learning to Change: An Information Perspective on Learning in the Organization," *Organization Science* 6, no. 5 (1995): 557–568.

Chapter 8

1. Richard Heeks, "Most-e-Government-for-Development Projects Fail. How Can Risks Be Reduced?" University of Manchester, UK, Institute for Development Policy and Management (2003), http://idpm.man.ac.uk/publications/wp/igov/educigov.shtml.
2. Gilda Garcia, interview with coauthor, January 28, 2012.
3. Harry Levinson, *Organizational Assessment: A Step-by-Step Guide to Effective Consulting* (Washington, D.C.: American Psychological Association, 2002), vii.
4. John P. Kretzmann and John L. McKnight, *Discovering Community Power: A Guide to Mobilizing Local Assets and Your Organization's Capacity* (Evanston, IL: ABCD Institute, 2005).
5. Chris Argyris and Donald Schon, *Theory in Practice: Increasing Professional Effectiveness* (San Francisco, CA: Jossey-Bass, 1974).
6. Ann K. Brooks, "Building Learning Organizations: The Individual-Culture Interaction," *Human Resource Development Quarterly* 3, no. 4 (1992): 323–336.
7. Edgar H. Schein, "The Role of the Founder in Creating Organizational Culture," *Organizational Dynamics* 12, no. 1 (1983): 22.
8. Ann K. Brooks, "Building Learning Organizations."
9. Iiris Aaltio-Marjosola, "From a 'Grand Story' to Multiple Narratives?," *Journal of Organizational Change Management* 7, no. 5 (1994): 56–68; Daniel Geiger and Elena Antonacopoulou, "Narratives and Organizational Dynamics: Exploring Blind Spots and Organizational Inertia," *The Journal of Applied Behavioral Science* 45, no. 3 (2009): 411–436; and Annalisa Murgia and Barbara Poggio, "Challenging Hegemonic Masculinities: Men's Stories on Gender Culture in Organizations," *Organization* 16, no. 3 (2009): 407–423.
10. Lovisa Näslund and Frida Pemer, "The Appropriated Language: Dominant Stories as a Source of Organizational Inertia," *Human Relations* 65, no. 89 (2012): 89–110.
11. Barry Oshry, *Leading Systems: Lessons from the Power Lab* (San Francisco, CA: Berrett-Koehler, 1999), 11.
12. Geary A. Rummler, Alan J. Ramias, and Richard A. Rummler, *White Space Revisited: Creating Value through Process* (San Francisco, CA: Jossey-Bass, 2010).
13. Brian Hindo, "At 3M, a Struggle between Efficiency and Creativity," *Business Week* (June 2007): 8–14.
14. John McKnight and Peter Block, *The Abundant Community: Awakening the Power of Families and Neighborhoods* (San Francisco, CA: Berrett-Koehler, 2010).

15. Julia Balogun, "From Blaming the Middle to Harnessing Its Potential: Creating Change Intermediaries," *British Journal of Management* 14 (2003): 69–83.
16. James M. Pappas and Bill Wooldridge, "Middle Managers' Divergent Strategic Activity: An Investigation of Multiple Measures of Network Centrality," *Journal of Management Studies* 44, no. 3. (2007): 323–341.
17. Cameron Anderson and Sandra E. Sparato, "Personality and Organizational Culture as Determinants of Influence," *Journal of Applied Psychology* 93, no. 3 (2008): 702–710.
18. Rob Cross and Robert J. Thomas, *Driving Results through Social Networks: How Top Organizations Leverage Networks for Performance and Growth* (San Francisco, CA: Jossey-Bass, 2009), 1.
19. David L. Cooperrider, Diana Whitney, and Jacqueline M. Stavros, *Appreciative Inquiry Handbook: The First in a Series of AI Workbooks for Leaders of Change* (Brunswick, OH: Crown Custom Publishing, 2003), 3.
20. Ibid., xviii.
21. John McKnight and Peter Block, 70.

Chapter 9

1. Zora Neale Hurston quoted in Valerie J. Janesick, *Stretching Exercises for Qualitative Researchers* (Thousand Oaks, CA: Sage, 2004), 1.
2. Carl Weick has written extensively on member sensemaking in organizations. In his book *Sensemaking in Organizations*, he has particularly highlighted the instances of ambiguity and uncertainty encountered.
3. Carl Sewell and Paul B. Brown, *Customers for Life: How to Turn That One-time Buyer into a Lifetime Customer* (New York: Doubleday Currency, 1990), 123.
4. Oscar Mink, personal conversation, Austin, TX, 1994.
5. James P. Spradley, *Participant Observation* (New York: Holt, Rinehart and Winston, 1980), 4–5.
6. Richard A. Krueger, *Focus Groups: A Practical Guide to Applied Research*, 2nd ed. (Thousand Oaks, CA: Sage, 1994), 11.
7. Tim Stapenhurst, *The Benchmarking Book: A How To Guide to Best Practices for Managers and Practitioners* (Oxford, UK: Butterworth-Heinemann by Elsevier, 2009), 6.
8. Matthew B. Miles and A. Michael Huberman, *Qualitative Data Analysis: An Expanded Sourcebook* (Thousand Oaks, CA: Sage, 1994), 11.
9. Amanda Coffey and Paul Atkinson, *Making Sense of Qualitative Data* (Thousand Oaks, CA: Sage, 1996), 10.
10. Yvonna S. Lincoln and Egon G. Guba list credibility, transferability, dependability, and confirmability. However, since consultant research is context and time specific, transferability, which refers to how well the findings can be transferred to other settings, and dependability, which refers to the extent of replicability, are of less relevance. See *Naturalistic Inquiry* (Beverly Hills, CA: Sage, 1985).

Bibliography

Aaltio-Marjosola, Iiris. "From a 'Grand Story' to Multiple Narratives?" *Journal of Organizational Change Management* 7, no. 5 (1994): 56–68.

Adolphs, Ralph. "Trust in the Brain." *Nature Neuroscience* 5, no. 3 (2002): 192–193.

Alston, John, and Isao Takei. *Japanese Business Culture and Practices: A Guide to Twenty-First Century Japanese Business.* Lincoln, NE: iUniverse, 2005.

Alvesson, Mats. "Knowledge Work: Ambiguity, Image and Identity." *Human Relations* 54, no. 7 (2001): 863–886.

Anderson, Cameron, and Sandra E. Sparato. "Personality and Organizational Culture as Determinants of Influence." *Journal of Applied Psychology* 93, no. 3 (2008): 702–710.

Argyris, Chris, and Donald Schon. *Theory in Practice: Increasing Professional Effectiveness.* San Francisco: Jossey-Bass, 1974.

Balogun, Julia. "From Blaming the Middle to Harnessing Its Potential: Creating Change Intermediaries." *British Journal of Management* 14 (2003): 69–83.

Barker, Albert E. "Remembering Reg Revans: Action Learning's Principal Pioneer." In *Action Learning: History and Evolution*, edited by Yury Boshyk and Robert Dilworth, 29–47. Basingstoke, Hampshire, UK: Palgrave Macmillan, 2010.

Barrett, Jean-Philippe, Lisa Feldman Laurenceau, and Paula R. Pietromonaco. "Intimacy as an Interpersonal Process: The Importance of Self-disclosure, Partner Disclosure, and Perceived Partner Responsiveness in Interpersonal Exchanges." *Journal of Personality and Social Psychology* 74, no. 5 (1998): 1238–1251.

Belenky, Mary F., et al. *Women's Ways of Knowing: The Development of Self, Voice, and Mind.* New York: Basic Books, 1986.

Biech, Elaine. *The Business of Consulting: The Basics and Beyond*, 2nd ed. San Francisco: Pfeiffer/John Wiley and Sons, 2007.

Block, Peter. *Flawless Consulting: A Guide to Getting Your Expertise Used.* San Francisco: Jossey-Bass/Pfeiffer, 2000.

Bogdanich, Walt. "The Radiation Boom: As Technology Surges, Radiation Safeguards Lag." *The New York Times*, January 26, 2010, http://www.nytimes.com/2010/01/27/us/27radiation.html?pagewanted = all&_r = 0.

Boshyk, Yury, and Robert Dilworth. *Action Learning: History and Evolution.* Basingstoke, Hampshire, UK: Palgrave Macmillan, 2010.

Brett, Jeanne, Kristin Behfar, and Mary C. Kern. "Managing Multicultural Teams." *Harvard Business Review* 84, no. 11 (2006): 84–91.

Brooks, Ann. "Power and the Production of Knowledge: Collective Team Learning in Work Organizations." *Human Resource Development Quarterly* 5, no. 4 (1994): 213–235.

Brooks, Ann, and Karen Watkins, eds. *The Emerging Power of Action Inquiry Technologies.* San Francisco: Jossey-Bass, 1994.

Brooks, Ann K. "Building Learning Organizations: The Individual-Culture Interaction." *Human Resource Development Quarterly* 3, no. 4 (1992): 323–336.

Brooks, Ann K., and Paul Kavanaugh. "Empowering the Surrounding Community." In *High-Performing Hispanic Schools: Creating Learning Communities*, edited by Pedro Reyes, Jay D. Scribner, and Alicia Paredes Scribner, 61–93. New York: Teachers College Press, 1999.

Cagney, Penelope. *Nonprofit Consulting Essentials: What Nonprofits and Consultants Need to Know*. Hoboken, NJ: John Wiley & Sons, Inc., 2010.

Campbell, W. Keith, et al. "Among Friends? An Examination of Friendship and the Self-Serving Bias." *British Journal of Social Psychology* 30 (2000): 229–239.

Coffey, Amanda, and Paul Atkinson. *Making Sense of Qualitative Data*. Thousand Oaks, CA: Sage, 1996.

Cohen, Jonathan D. "The Vulcanization of the Human Brain: A Neural Perspective on Interactions between Cognition and Emotion." *Journal of Economic Perspectives* 19, no. 40 (2005): 3–24.

Collins, Jim. "Level 5 Leadership: The Triumph of Humility and Fierce Resolve." *Harvard Business Review* 83, no. 7/8 (2001): 67–77.

———. *Good to Great: Why Some Companies Make the Leap . . . and Others Don't*. New York: Harper Collins, 2001.

Cooperrider, David L. "Appreciative Inquiry: Toward a Methodology for Understanding and Enhancing Organizational Innovation." PhD diss., Case Western Reserve University, 1986.

Cooperrider, David L., and Diana Whitney. *Appreciative Inquiry: A Positive Revolution in Change*. San Francisco: Berrett-Koehler, 2005.Cooperrider, David L., Diana Whitney, and Jacqueline M. Stavros. *Appreciative Inquiry Handbook: The First in a Series of AI Workbooks for Leaders of Change*. Brunswick, OH: Crown Custom Publishing, 2003.

Cozolino, Louis. *The Neuroscience of Human Relationships: Attachment and the Developing Social Brain*. New York: W.W. Norton, 2006.

Cross, Rob, and Robert J. Thomas. *Driving Results through Social Networks: How Top Organizations Leverage Networks for Performance and Growth*. San Francisco: Jossey-Bass, 2009.

Curnow, Barry, and Jonathan Reuvid. *International Guide to Management Consultancy: The Evolution, Practice and Structure of Management Consultancy Worldwide*, 2nd ed. London: Kogan Page, 2006.

De Haan, Erik. *Fearless Consulting: Temptations, Risks and Limits of the Profession*. Chichester, West Sussex, UK: John Wiley & Sons, 2006.

Dewey, John. *Democracy and Education*. New York: The Macmillan Company, 1916.

———. *Logic—The Theory of Inquiry*. New York: Henry Holt and Co., 1938.

Donne, John. *The Works of John Donne, Vol. III*. Edited by Henry Alford. London: John W. Parker, 1839.

Dreier, Peter. "Katrina and Power in America." *Urban Affairs Review* 41, no. 4 (2006): 528–549.

Edersheim, Elizabeth Haas. *McKinsey's Marvin Bower: Vision, Leadership & the Creation of Management Consulting*. Hoboken, NJ: John Wiley & Sons, 2004.

Edmondson, Amy. "Psychological Safety and Learning Behavior in Work Teams." *Administrative Science Quarterly* 44, no. 2 (1999): 350–383.

Edmondson, Amy C. "Managing the Risk of Learning: Psychological Safety in Work Teams." In *International Handbook of Organizational Teamwork and Cooperative Working*, edited by Dean Tjosvold, Michael A. West, and Ken G. Smith, 255–276. Hoboken, NJ: Wiley, 2003.

Eggers, Dave. *A Hologram for the King*. San Francisco: McSweeney's, 2012.

Einstein, Albert. *The Ultimate Quotable Einstein*. Edited by Alice Calaprice. Princeton, NJ: Princeton University Press and the Hebrew University of Jerusalem, 2011.

Eisenhower, Dwight D. "Remarks." National Defense Executive Reserve Conference, Washington, DC, November 14, 1957. http://www.presidency.ucsb.edu/ws/?pid = 10951.

Eliot, Thomas S. *Shakespeare and the Stoicism of Seneca*. London: Oxford University Press, 1927.

Engeström, Yrjö, Reijo Miettinen, and Raija-Leena Punamäki-Gitai, eds. *Perspectives on Activity Theory*. Cambridge, UK: Cambridge University Press, 1999.
Ess, Charles. "Liberal Arts and Distance Education: Can Socratic Virtue (*arete*) and Confucius' Exemplary Person (*junzi*) Be Taught Online?" In *Brave New Classrooms: Educational Democracy and the Internet*, edited by Mark Pegrum and Joe Lockard, 189–212. New York: Peter Lang, 2007.
Fineman, Stephen, ed. *The Emotional Organization: Passions and Power*. Oxford, UK: Blackwell Publishing, 2008.
Fombrun, Charles J., and Daniel F. Oriesek. "The Advice Business: The Industry of Consulting." In *The Advice Business: Essential Tools and Models for Management Consulting*. Upper Saddle River, NJ: Pearson/Prentice-Hall, 2004.
Friedman, Thomas L. "Collaborate vs. Collaborate." *The New York Times*, January 12, 2013. http://www.nytimes.com/2013/01/13/opinion/sunday/friedman-collaborate-vs-collaborate.html?_r = 0.
Friedman, Victor J., and Ariane Berthoin Antal. "Negotiating Reality: A Theory of Action Approach to Intercultural Competence." *Management Learning* 36, no. 1 (2005): 70.
Gadsden-Ross, Helen. "Knowledge Deficit: What's the Effect on the New Employee?" PhD diss. proposal, Texas State University, 2012.
Geiger, Daniel, and Elena Antonacopoulou. "Narratives and Organizational Dynamics: Exploring Blind Spots and Organizational Inertia." *The Journal of Applied Behavioral Science* 45, no. 3 (2009): 411–436.
Gibbons, Michael, et al. *The New Production of Knowledge: The Dynamics of Science and Research in Contemporary Societies*. London: Sage, 1994.
Gilligan, Carol C. *In a Different Voice*. Cambridge, MA: Harvard University Press, 1982.
Goenka, S. N. "The Art of Living: Vipassana Meditation." *Vipassana Meditation Website*. http://www.dhamma.org/en/art.shtml (accessed August 17, 2012).
Goleman, Daniel. *Destructive Emotions: How Can We Overcome Them?: A Scientific Dialogue with the Dalai Lama, Narrated by Daniel Goleman*. New York: Bantam, 2004.
Graham, Ian. "The Compleat Requirements Analyst." *IEEE Software* 20, no. 6 (2003): 99–101.
Gratton, Lynda, and Tamara J. Erickson. "Eight Ways to Build Collaborative Teams." In *Harvard Business Review on Collaborating Effectively*, 37–64. Boston: Harvard Business School Publishing Corporation, 2011.
Greenleaf, Robert K. *Servant Leadership: A Journey into the Nature of Legitimate Power and Greatness*. Mahwah, NJ: Paulist Press, 2002.
Grove, Cornelius N., and Grovewell Global Leadership Solutions LLC. *Introduction to the GLOBE Research Project on Leadership Worldwide*, 2005. http://www.grovewell.com/pub-GLOBE-intro.html (accessed September 9, 2012).
Hampden-Turner, Charles, and Fons Trompenaars. *Riding the Waves of Culture: Understanding Diversity in Global Business*. New York: McGraw-Hill, 1997.
Hatfield, Elaine, John T. Cacioppo, and Richard L. Rapson. *Emotional Contagion*. New York: Cambridge University Press, 1994.
Heatherton, Todd F. "Neuroscience of Self and Self-regulation." *Annual Review of Psychology* 62 (2011): 363–390.
Heeks, Richard. "Most-e-Government-for-Development Projects Fail. How Can Risks Be Reduced?" *University of Manchester, UK, Institute for Development Policy and Management*, 2003. http://idpm.man.ac.uk/publications/wp/igov/educigov.shtml (accessed August 7, 2012).
Hennock, Mary. "News Analysis: China Looks to Western Partners to Reshape Its Universities." *The Chronicle of Higher Education*, July 17, 2011, http://chronicle.com.libproxy.txstate.edu/article/News-Analysis-China-Looks-to/128222/.
Hetherington, Rian. *Realizing Change: Vipassana Meditation in Action*. Seattle, WA: Pariyatti Press, 2003.
Hindo, Brian. "At 3M, a Struggle between Efficiency and Creativity." *Business Week*, June 11 (2007): 8–14.

Hirshleifer, David, and Tyler Shumway. "Good Day Sunshine: Stock Market Returns and the Weather." *Journal of Finance* 58 (2003): 1009–1032.
Hofstede, Geert. *Culture's Consequences: International Differences in Work-related Values*. Beverly Hills, CA: Sage, 1980.
Hofstede, Geert, Gert Jan Hofstede, and Michael Minkov. *Cultures and Organizations: Software for the Mind*, 3rd ed. New York: McGraw-Hill, 2010.
Hong, Ying, et al. "Multicultural Minds: A Dynamic Constructivist Approach to Culture and Cognition." *American Psychologist* 55, no. 7 (2000): 709–720.
Hoppe, Michael H., and the Center for Creative Leadership. *Active Listening: Improve Your Ability to Listen and Lead*. San Francisco: Pfeiffer, 2011.
Ihlwan, Moon. "Camp Samsung." *BusinessWeek*, July 3, 2006, 46.
Izard, Carroll E. "Emotion Theory and Research: Highlights, Unanswered Questions, and Emerging Issues." *Annual Review of Psychology* 60 (2009): 1–25.
Jha, Amishi P., Jason Krompinger, and Michael J. Baime. "Mindfulness Training Modifies Subsystems of Attention." *Cognitive Affective Behavioral Neuroscience* 7, no. 2 (2007): 109–119.
Kahneman, Daniel. "Maps of Bounded Rationality: A Perspective on Intuitive Judgment and Choice." Nobel Prize Lecture, Aula Magna, Stockholm University, Stockholm, Sweden, December 8, 2002.
Kegan, Robert. *In Over Our Heads: The Mental Demands of Modern Life*. Cambridge, MA: Harvard University Press, 1994.
Kiefer, Tina. "Feeling Bad: Antecedents and Consequences of Negative Emotions in Ongoing Change." *Organizational Behavior* 26, no. 8 (2005): 875–897.
Klein, Karen E. "Smart Answers: Why Self-Employed Consultants Fail." *Bloomberg Businessweek: Small Business*, May 10, 2011. http://www.businessweek.com/smallbiz/content/may2011/sb2011059_763239.html.
Klinenberg, Eric. "Denaturalizing Disaster: A Social Autopsy of the 1995 Chicago Heat Wave." *Theory and Society* 28 (1999) 239–295.
Kretzmann, John P., and John L. McKnight. *Building Communities from the Inside Out: A Path toward Finding and Mobilizing a Community's Assets*. Chicago: ACTA Publications, 1993.
———. *Discovering Community Power: A Guide to Mobilizing Local Assets and Your Organization's Capacity*. Evanston, IL: ABCD Institute, 2005.
Krueger, Richard A. *Focus Groups: A Practical Guide to Applied Research*, 2nd ed. Thousand Oaks, CA: Sage, 1994.
Kubr, Milan, and Martin Kubr, eds. *Management Consulting: A Guide to the Profession*. Geneva, Switzerland: International Labour Office, 2002.
Kuhn, Martin. *House of Lies: How Management Consultants Steal Your Watch and Then Tell You the Time*. New York: Warner Business Books, 2005.
Langer, Ellen J., and Mihnea Moldoveanu. "Mindfulness Research and the Future." *Journal of Social Issues* 56, no. 1 (2000): 1–9.
Lave, Jean. *Situated Learning: Legitimate Peripheral Participation*. Cambridge, UK: Cambridge University Press, 1991.
Lave, Jean, and Etienne Wenger. *Situated Learning: Legitimate Peripheral Participation*. Cambridge, UK: Cambridge University Press, 1991.
Leary, Mark R., and Roy F. Baumeister, "The Nature and Function of Self-Esteem: Sociometer Theory." In *Advances in Experimental Social Psychology*, edited by Mark P. Zanna, 1–62. New York: Academic Press, 2000.
Leistner, Frank. *Mastering Organizational Knowledge Flow: How to Make Knowledge Sharing Work*. Hoboken, NJ: Wiley and SAS, 2010.
Lerner, Jennifer S., et al. "Effects of Fear and Anger on Perceived Risks of Terrorism: A National Field Experiment." *Psychological Science* 14 (2003): 144–150.
Lerner, Jennifer S., Deborah A. Small, and George Loewenstein. "Heart Strings and Purse Strings: Carryover Effects of Emotions on Economic Decisions." *Psychological Science* 15, no. 5 (May 2004): 337–341.

Levinson, Harry. *Organizational Assessment: A Step-by-Step Guide to Effective Consulting*. Washington, DC: American Psychological Association, 2002.

Lewin, Kurt. *Resolving Social Conflicts: Selected Papers on Group Dynamics*. Edited by Gertrude W. Lewin. New York: Harper and Row, 1948.

Lincoln, Yvonna S., and Egon G. Guba. *Naturalistic Inquiry*. Beverly Hills, CA: Sage, 1985.

Lipshitz, Raanan, Gary Klein, Judith Orasanu, and Edward Salas. "Taking Stock of Naturalistic Decision Making." *Journal of Behavioral Decision Making* 14, no. 5 (2001): 331–352.

Lozano, Reynaldo G. "A Socio-technical Analysis of Knowledgeable Practice in Radiation Therapy." PhD diss., Texas State University, 2012.

Lundberg, Craig C., and Cheri A. Young. "A Note on Emotions and Consultancy." *Journal of Organizational Change Management* 14, no. 6 (2001): 530–538.

MacDonald, Stuart. "Learning to Change: An Information Perspective on Learning in the Organization." *Organization Science* 6, no. 5 (1995): 557–568.

Maister, David H., Charles H. Green, and Robert M. Galford. *The Trusted Advisor*. New York: Free Press, 2000.

Marquardt, Michael. *Leading with Questions: How Leaders Find the Right Solutions by Knowing What to Ask*. San Francisco: Jossey-Bass, 2005.

Martineau, Jennifer, and Kelly Hannum. *Evaluating the Impact of Leadership Development: A Professional Guide*. Greensboro, NC: Center for Creative Leadership, Greensboro, NC, 2001.

McKnight, John, and Peter Block. *The Abundant Community: Awakening the Power of Families and Neighborhoods*. San Francisco: Berrett-Koehler, 2012.

McSweeney, Brendan. "Hofstede's Model of National Cultural Differences and Consequences: A Triumph of Faith—A Failure of Analysis." *Human Relations* 55, no. 1 (2002): 89–118.

Merron, Keith. *Consulting Mastery: How the Best Make the Biggest Difference*. San Francisco: Berrett-Koehler, 2005.

Michel, Daryl Allan. "An Analysis of Faculty Meeting Content and Processes: A Multi-case Study of Three South Texas Schools." PhD diss., Texas State University, 2011.

Miles, Matthew B., and A. Michael Huberman. *Qualitative Data Analysis: An Expanded Sourcebook*. Thousand Oaks, CA: Sage, 1994.

Murgia, Annalisa, and Barbara Poggio. "Challenging Hegemonic Masculinities: Men's Stories on Gender Culture in Organizations." *Organization* 16, no. 3 (2009): 407–423.

Näslund, Lovisa, and Frida Pemer. "The Appropriated Language: Dominant Stories as a Source of Organizational Inertia." *Human Relations* 65, no. 89 (2012): 89–110.

Neff, Kristin D. "Development and Validation of a Scale to Measure Self-Compassion." *Self and Identity* 2 (2003): 223–250.

———. "Self-Compassion: An Alternative Conceptualization of a Healthy Attitude Toward Oneself." *Self and Identity* 2 (2003): 85–102.

Neff, Kristin D., and Roos Vonk. "Self-Compassion versus Global Self-Esteem: Two Different Ways of Relating to Oneself." *Journal of Personality* 77, no. 1 (2009): 23–50.

Nehru, Jawaharlal. *Visit to America*. New York: J. Day Co., 1950.

Nonaka, Ikujiro, and Tokyo Hirotaka. *The Knowledge-creating Company: How Japanese Companies Create the Dynamics of Innovation*. New York: Oxford University Press, 1995.

O'Neil, Judy, and Victoria Marsick. *Understanding Action Learning*. Washington, DC: AOM, 2007.

Oshry, Barry. *Leading Systems: Lessons from the Power Lab*. San Francisco: Berrett-Koehler, 1999.

Pappas, James M., and Bill Wooldridge. "Middle Managers' Divergent Strategic Activity: An Investigation of Multiple Measures of Network Centrality." *Journal of Management Studies* 44, no. 3. (2007): 323–341.

Patnaik, Dev. "Viewpoint: Empathy Is Growth." *Bloomberg Business: Innovation and Design*, March 4, 2009. *http://www.businessweek.com/innovate/content/mar2009/id2009034_766385.htm*.

Peterson, Christopher, and Martin Seligman. *Character Strengths and Virtues: A Handbook and Classification*. New York: Oxford University Press, 2004.

Phelan, Karen. *I'm Sorry I Broke Your Company*. San Francisco: Berrett-Koehler, 2013.

Pillay, Srinivasan S. *Your Brain and Business: The Neuroscience of Great Leaders*. Upper Saddle River, NJ: Pearson Education/FT Press, 2011.

Pinault, Lewis. *Consulting Demons: Inside the Unscrupulous World of Global Corporate Consulting*. New York: Harper Collins, 2001.

Polanyi, Michael. *The Tacit Dimension*. Chicago: University of Chicago Press, 1966.

Porter, Michael E., and Mark R. Kramer. "Creating Shared Value: How to Reinvent Capitalism and Unleash a Wave of Innovation." *Harvard Business Review* 89, no. 1/2 (2011): 62–77.

Pugh, S. Douglas. "Service with a Smile: Emotional Contagion in the Service Encounter." *Academy of Management Journal* 44, no. 5 (2001): 1018–1027.

Pyszczynski, Tom, Jeff Greenberg, Sheldon Solomon, Jamie Arndt, and Jeff Schimel. "Why Do People Need Self-Esteem? A Theoretical and Empirical Review." *Psychological Bulletin* 130, no. 3 (2004): 435–468.

Reason, Peter, and Hillary Bradbury, eds. *Handbook of Action Research: Participative Inquiry and Practice*. Thousand Oaks, CA: Sage, 2001.

Redlmeier, Donald A., and Simon D. Baxter. "Rainy Weather and Medical School Admission Interviews." *Canadian Medical Association Journal* 181 (2009): 933.

Reiss, Helen. "Commentary | Empathy in Medicine—A Neurobiological Perspective." *Journal of the American Medical Association* 304, no. 14: 1604–1605.

Reiss, Helen, et al. "Empathy Training for Resident Physicians: A Randomized Controlled Trial of a Neuroscience-Informed Curriculum." *Journal of General Internal Medicine* 26, no. 10 (2011): 1280–1286.

Revans, Reg. *ABC of Action Learning*. London: Gower, 2011.

Rummler, Geary A., Alan J. Ramias, and Richard A. Rummler. *White Space Revisited: Creating Value through Process*. San Francisco: Jossey-Bass, 2010.

Salas, Edwardo, Michael A. Rosen, and Deborah DiazGranados. "Expertise-based Intuition and Decision Making in Organizations." *Journal of Management* 36, no. 4 (2010): 941–973.

Sanker, Dan. *Collaborate: The Art of We*. Hoboken, NJ: John Wiley, 2012.

Saporito, Bill. "The Conspiracy to End Cancer." *Time Magazine*, April 4, 2013, http://healthland.time.com/2013/04/01/the-conspiracy-to-end-cancer/.

Schaefer, Carol. *Grandmothers Counsel the World: Women Elders Offer Their Vision for Our Planet*. Boston: Trumpeter Press, 2006.

Schaffer, Robert. *High Impact Consulting: How Clients and Consultants Can Work Together to Achieve Extraordinary Results*, 2nd ed. San Francisco: Jossey-Bass, 2002.

Schein, Edgar H. "The Role of the Founder in Creating Organizational Culture." *Organizational Dynamics* 12, no. 1 (1983): 13–28.

———. *Process Consultation: Its Role in Organization Development, Volume 1*. New York: Prentice Hall, 1988.

———. "The Concept of Client from a Process Consultation Perspective: A Guide for Change Agents." MIT, Sloan School of Management working paper #3946–97, Cambridge, MA, March 1997.

———. *Process Consultation Revisited: Building the Helping Relationship*. Reading, MA: Addison-Wesley, 1999.

———. *Helping: How to Offer, Give, and Receive Help*. San Francisco: Berrett-Kohler, 2009.

Schein, Edgar H., Adam Kahane, and Adam Scharmer. "Humility and Ignorance: What It Takes to Be an Effective Process Consultant." *Reflections* 3, no. 2 (2001): 8–19.

Schrecker, Ted. "Denaturalizing Scarcity: A Strategy of Enquiry for Public-Health Ethics." *Bulletin of the World Health Organization* 86, no. 8 (2008): 600–695.

Schon, Donald. *The Reflective Practitioner: How Professionals Think in Action*. New York: Basic Books, 1983.

Schwarz, Mirela, and Timothy Clark. "Clients' Different Moves in Managing the Client-Consultant Relationship." In *Client-Consultant Collaboration: Coping with Complexity and Change*, edited by Anthony F. Buono and Flemming Poulfelt, 3–28. Charlotte, NC: Information Age Publishing, 2009.

Schwartz, Norbert. "Feelings-as-Information Theory." In *Handbook of Theories of Social Psychology: Volume One*, edited by Paul A. M. Van Lange et al., 289–308. Thousand Oaks, CA: Sage, 2011.

Scriven, Michael. *Evaluation Thesaurus*. Thousand Oaks, CA: Sage, 1991.

Sewell, Carl, and Paul B. Brown. *Customers for Life: How to Turn That One-time Buyer into a Lifetime Customer*. New York: Doubleday Currency, 1990.

Siegel, Daniel J. *The Developing Mind: How Relationships and the Brain Interact to Shape Who We Are*. New York: Guilford Press, 1999.

Simon, Alan, and Vanya Kumar. "Clients' Views on Strategic Capabilities Which Lead to Management Consulting Success." *Management Decision* 39, no. 5 (2001): 362–372.

Solomon, Robert C. *A Better Way to Think about Business*. New York: Oxford University Press, 1999.

Sorensen, Peter, et al. "Consulting in the Middle East: Recent Experiences and Alternative Models." Paper presented at the Professional Development Workshop, Academy of Management, Boston, MA, August 3–7, 2012.

Spradley, James P. *Participant Observation*. New York: Holt, Rinehart and Winston, 1980.

Stanovich, Keith E., and Richard F. West. "Individual Differences in Reasoning: Implications for the Rationality Debate." *Behavioral and Brain Sciences* 23, no. 5 (2000): 645–726.

Stapenhurst, Tim. *The Benchmarking Book: A How To Guide to Best Practices for Managers and Practitioners*. Oxford, UK: Butterworth-Heinemann by Elsevier, 2009.

Stroh, Linda K., and Homer H. Johnson. *The Basic Principles of Effective Consulting*. Mahwah, NJ: Lawrence Erlbaum Associates, 2006.

Sturdy, Andrew. "Popular Critiques of Consultancy and a Politics of Management Learning?" *Management Learning* 40, no. 4 (2009): 258–259.

Tangney, June P. "Humility: Theoretical Perspectives, Empirical Findings and Directions for Future Research." *Journal of Social and Clinical Psychology* 19, no. 1 (2000): 70–82.

———. "Humility." In *Handbook of Positive Psychology*, edited by C. R. Snyder and Shane J. Lopez, 411–422. New York: Oxford University Press, 2002.

Thanissaro, Bhikkhu. "The Path of Concentration & Mindfulness." *Access to Insight* 8 (March 2011). http://www.accesstoinsight.org/lib/authors/thanissaro/concmind.html (Accessed March 12, 2012).

Thompson, Leigh L. *The Mind and Heart of the Negotiator*, 5th ed. Upper Saddle River, NJ: Pearson Education, 2012.

Tice, Dianne M., et al. "When Modesty Prevails: Differential Favorability of Self-Presentation to Friends and Strangers." *Journal of Personality and Social Psychology* 69 (1995): 1120–1138.

Trist, Eric L., and Kenneth W. Bamforth. "Some Social and Psychological Consequences of the Longwall Method of Coal Getting: An Examination of the Psychological Situation and Defences of a Work Group in Relation to the Social Structure and Technological Content of the Work System." *Human Relations* 4, no. 3 (1951): 3–38.

Vera, Dusya, and Antonio Rodriguez-Lopez. "Strategic Virtues: Humility as a Source of Competitive Advantage." *Organizational Dynamics* 33, no. 4 (2004): 393–408.

Warren, James R. "Predicting and Enhancing Client Success." In *Creative Consulting*, edited by Anthony E. Buono, 345–370. Greenwich, CT: Information Age Publishing, 2004.

Weick, Karl E. *Sensemaking in Organizations*. Thousand Oaks, CA: Sage, 1995.

Weick, Karl E., and Ted Putnam. "Organizing for Mindfulness: Eastern Wisdom and Western Knowledge." *Journal of Management Inquiry* 15, no. 3 (2006): 275–287.

Wen, Leana, and Joshua Kosowski. *When Doctors Don't Listen: How to Avoid Misdiagnoses and Unnecessary Tests*. New York: St. Martin's Press, 2013.

Wertsch, James, V. *The Concept of Activity in Soviet Psychology*. Armonk, NY: M.E. Sharpe, 1981.

Westen, Drew, et al., "Neural Bases of Motivated Reasoning: An FMRI Study of Emotional Constraints on Partisan Political Judgment in the 2004 U.S. Presidential Election." *Journal of Cognitive Neuroscience* 18, no. 1 (2006): 1947–1958.

Williams, Elba. "The Perspectives of Latina Immigrant Mothers of Children in the Public Schools." Unpublished data, Texas State University, 2012.

Woolley, Anita Williams, Christopher F. Chabris, Alex Pentland, Nada Hashmi, and Thomas W. Malone. "Evidence for a Collective Intelligence Factor in the Performance of Human Groups." *Science* 330, no. 6004 (2010): 686–688.

Zaki, Jamil, Jochen Weber, Niall Bolger, and Kevin Ochsner. "The Neural Bases of Empathic Accuracy." *Proceedings of the National Academy of Science of the USA* 106, no. 27 (2009): 11382–11387.

Zaki, Jamil, and Kevin Ochsner. "The Neuroscience of Empathy: Progress, Pitfalls and Promise." *Nature Neuroscience* 15 (2012): 675–680.

Zhu, Ying, et al. "Neural Basis of Cultural Influence on Self-Representation." *NeuroImage* 34, no. 3 (2007): 1310–1316.

Index

Please note: page numbers in *italics* indicate figures, tables, and boxes